HISTORIC CHICAGO *Bakeries*

HISTORIC CHICAGO *Bakeries*

JENNIFER BILLOCK

Published by American Palate
A Division of The History Press
Charleston, SC
www.historypress.com

Front cover, clockwise from top: Roeser's Bakery; Library of Congress; Alpha Baking Company; Ferrara Bakery; Alpha Baking Company.
Back cover: Gonnella Baking Company; *inset*: Thomas Hawk.

First published 2021

Manufactured in the United States

ISBN 9781467150118

Library of Congress Control Number: 2021941611

Notice: The information in this book is true and complete to the best of our knowledge. It is offered without guarantee on the part of the author or The History Press. The author and The History Press disclaim all liability in connection with the use of this book.

For Aunt Joyce. Miss you every day.

Contents

Acknowledgements

Thank you to all of the bakery owners and employees who so generously offered me some of their time. I loved every second of our conversations and behind-the-scenes tours and am forever grateful for all the sweet treats and breads you allowed me to enjoy.

Thank you to my friends and family for putting up with me while I wrote yet another book. And to all those who helped me eat all the baked goods I brought home, you're welcome.

Thank you to my stellar team at The History Press; you all make writing these books a painless, easy and fun process. Ben, if you're ever back in Chicago, I'll take you to my favorite places.

Special thanks to all the Chicagoans who shared their input on which bakeries to include and also to the following bakery owners and employees: Heidi Hedeker; Meg McDonnell; Nella and Nello; Stephanie Powell, Michael Thornburg and your fun co-worker whose name I sadly can't recall; John Roeser; Ozzie Ocegueda; Martin Flores; Norm Dinkel; Peter Rios; Mike and Becky Weber; Guy and Jory Downer; Joe Boehm and Pam; Can Lao; Toni DeWitt; Linda Ahern; Anthony Rubino; Bill and Kim Goebel; and Fred Pecoraro. Thanks also to Friends of the Pullman State Historic Site.

Introduction

Any multigenerational Chicago family is bound to have a family bakery. Not one that they own, of course, but one that they've been going to for generations. For me, it's Weber's Bakery. Their banana split torte has been a staple at family gatherings for as long as I can remember. When I moved to the north side, my bakery—and the one I share with my friends and partner—became Dinkel's. Chicagoans are fiercely loyal to their neighborhood bakeries, even returning to the ones they left for generations after moving away.

That loyalty and, indeed, territoriality are part of Chicago's identity. From the time the city was founded in 1833, immigrants coming to Chicago settled in pockets, staying with their own communities. With that came distinct neighborhoods and different lifestyles in each—whether it was Little Italy, Greektown, Irish enclaves on the south side, Little India, Swede Town, German settlements on the north side, Polish families in the west and more. And every neighborhood had its own ethnic bakery, sometimes multiple. The names of those neighborhoods and the businesses within have changed over the years, but the distinctions are still there, creating seventy-seven official neighborhoods and dozens of unofficial ones. Today, when you tell someone you live in Chicago, you're almost immediately asked what part of the city you're from. We want to know which neighborhood you're in; we want to know where your parents grew up; we want to know where you like to eat and what bakery you prefer. To me, that says volumes about civic pride and the curiosity of Chicagoans to continually learn about their home and the people in it.

Baking history in Chicago runs just as deep as our family ties and pride in the area. At one time, about seven thousand bakeries dotted the city streets. The Retail Bakers of America association was founded here. The American Institute of Baking was here. National names like Sara Lee and Eli's got their starts in Chicago. Even the brownie was invented here, by Bertha Palmer of the Palmer House Hilton fame. We have our own regional desserts and treats as well, regional not just to Chicago but to different sides of Chicago, that you'll learn about as you read this book.

Sadly, the scratch-made multigenerational family bakery is a dying breed. By the early 1990s, the number of bakeries in Chicago dipped down to only 444, and now there are even fewer. Home kitchens grew and expanded, and grocery store bakeries and budget brands took over, pushing out the mom-and-pop establishments that sold everything fresh first thing in the morning, with no preservatives and instead with a hefty helping of love for their craft. These bakeries have defined our food traditions, whether it's an atomic cake for family celebrations, bacon buns in the morning, a poppy seed bun for our hot dogs, pączki and zeppole for holidays or (in the never-ending Chicago debate) seeded or unseeded rye bread.

This book takes you through a chronological history of bakeries in Chicago, organized by opening date of the business. You'll learn about the bakery, what it sold, its customers and fun historical nuggets. To be considered for inclusion, bakeries needed to have opened fifty years ago or earlier. It's impossible to include them all—this book would be much thicker if it included all of the thousands of bakeries from the city's past—so the ones included are historic, well known and much loved. There are necessarily some omissions of some beloved bakeries; recommendations for ones to include continued hitting my inbox until the moment this manuscript was submitted. With that in mind, I want to pay homage to some of the spots that didn't get their time in the limelight in this book: Eli's Cheesecake, which is fairly well covered in The History Press book *Iconic Chicago Dishes, Drinks, and Desserts*; Archway; Cliff's; Cora's and their heart-shaped Valentine's Day cakes; Diamond Kosher; Fred's; Hamlin; Hendle's; Hoffman's; Ingram's Busy Bee; Janssen's; Jarosch; Sara Lee Corporation; Lawrence Bakery; Norn's; Nyberg's, which was in operation for about forty years; Oven Fresh; Palermo; Phillip's; Prince's; Pulaski Bakery; Rolla Brothers; Rolnick's; Rosner's; Sandowski's; Sanitary Bakery; Selke's; Sheldon Heights; Tel-Aviv Kosher Bakery, which has been around since the 1950s; Thompson's; Village Bake Shop and its sponsored polka radio station; Schmeissing's, which was in operation for fifty-four years; Schlegl's; Chiu Quon Bakery, the oldest bakery in Chinatown; and Wasilauski's, known at the time for its bowling team.

With few exceptions, the bakeries listed in this book are contained within the city limits. Those included from outside the city either have Chicago beginnings or particular notoriety with locals living near the edge of town. When available, the address of the bakery's last known location is noted.

I

1880s to 1910s

By 1880, Chicago had 503,000 residents. That number quadrupled, to more than 2 million, by 1910. The bakeries in this section are some of the original ones, the ones that laid the foundation for future generations. They were founded by immigrants who were typically master bakers in their home countries. Here, we find a lot of breads, savory baked goods, hyper-regional specialty desserts and the beginnings of a robust sweets industry in Chicago.

These spots represented their communities to the letter—too early for soon-to-be-iconic treats, but rather representing a snapshot of the homeland. They also literally emerged from the ashes. The Great Chicago Fire decimated the community in 1871, unfortunately taking many records of the earliest bakeries in the city along with it. We know that Chicago founder Jean Baptiste Point DuSable and his wife owned a bakehouse by the Chicago River in the 1700s and that flour milling became a big industry here in the 1830s. In 1880, Chicago began officially licensing its bakeries.

These shops were some of those—in addition to being a fresh start. They served not only new immigrants to the United States but also Chicagoans rebuilding the urban landscape after the fire.

H.H. KOHLSAAT AND COMPANY

Multiple Locations

The modern-day lunch counter might not exist if it weren't for Herman Henry (H.H.) Kohlsaat and his chain of bakeries. He moved to Chicago in 1865, taking a job with wholesale bakery Blake, Shaw and Company. By 1883, he had married Blake's daughter and bought the business. H.H. Kohlsaat and Company was known for bakery lunch establishments, places where businessmen in the Loop could sit down at a counter for a quick lunch and bite of cake. As business grew, he opened several locations and became one of the largest bakery companies in the city, selling bread wholesale for five cents a loaf.

Kohlsaat often fought with the unions and refused to join them. One incident in the later years of his business had the entire staff strike for seven weeks in a move that made Kohlsaat believe the Master Bakers' Association was part of a larger conspiracy to force him to join the union. More than seventy employees were out of work.

The H.H. Kohlsaat Bakery Company building in the early twentieth century. *Newberry Library.*

H.H. Kohlsaat.
Library of Congress.

In 1891, Kohlsaat sold off his bakeries and restaurants to the City of Chicago when he decided to go into journalism and politics. City officials then used the bakeries to experiment with healthy and inexpensive meals for public school children. *The New York Times* reported at the time that the bakery was so successful that it became something of a cook's university; menus were always published a day in advance, and local wealthy homeowners would come down with their cooks so they could learn how to make all the recipes.

Kohlsaat moved from baking to publishing. He owned several newspapers and wrote two books. He started by purchasing half-interest in the *Chicago Inter-Ocean* and then sold that to buy the *Chicago Times-Herald* and the *Evening Post*, which he converted from Democratic papers to Republican ones. From there, he purchased the *Chicago Record* and the *Times-Herald*, combining the two papers into a single one called the *Record-Herald.* After that, he went back to the *Inter-Ocean* for a year and then left to become a staffer at *The New York Times.*

Kohlsaat didn't just popularize the lunch counter meal; he also invented something unique: the comics section of newspapers. Most credit Joseph Pulitzer with the invention, but Kohlsaat launched the first with his *Inter-Ocean Illustrated Supplement* in 1892. It was an eight-page tabloid filled with full-color features, fiction and miscellany. This was the first time an American newspaper had a color supplement, and in 1893, Pulitzer replicated the effort in New York.

Meanwhile, Kohlsaat was out in the community in Chicago, helping organize the 1893 World's Columbian Exposition; creating and running the first ever car race in the United States in 1895; campaigning for Republican interests and befriending Republican dignitaries; and writing books on his political exploits.

Kohlsaat died in 1924 at the Washington, D.C. home of Herbert Hoover, who would become president in five years' time. Kohlsaat was in town to attend the World Series with Hoover and suffered what appeared to be either a heart attack or a deadly stroke. A memorial tablet for him is in the Washington National Cathedral.

GONNELLA BAKING COMPANY

Multiple Locations

Say the name Gonnella to anyone in Chicago, and they'll immediately think of bread—crispy crusts, tender interiors, the delightful smell of Vienna bread (a product original to the first bakery), French bread, Italian bread and individually wrapped hot dog buns. Gonnella is a legacy business in Chicago.

In 1886, Allesandro Gonnella and his sister came to Chicago from Italy. He took a job working in a local bakery on DeKoven Street, down in the basement of a three-flat with a single brick wood-burning oven. Shortly after he started there, the owners decided to sell the bakery. Gonnella loved the work so much that he sent away to Italy, asking for help to buy and run the bakery.

"Think, at the time, it wasn't picking up the phone," said Meg McDonnell, Gonnella's vice president of marketing and a member of the founding family. "It wasn't sending a text. This probably took months to get the word back to Italy and then get people back."

Gonnella bakers removing freshly baked bread from the tunnel oven by peel board and putting them on racks to cool. *Gonnella Baking Company.*

Left: The original neon sign from Gonnella's Erie Street production plant, from the 1950s to the 1960s. It's now in Schaumburg and fully functioning. *Gonnella Baking Company.*

Below: Fresh baked bread in Gonnella's shipping room on Erie Street, ready to go on route trucks, circa 1940s. *Gonnella Baking Company.*

> Meg McDonnell on the Family Community at Work in Chicago
>
> My favorite memory is just working with family. It's really hard sometimes, because it's family, but at the same time, not everybody gets to see their cousin Bob at the office every day. And not everybody gets to see cousin Tom's daughter come to work there. There's love for the people you are working with, whether they be family or not. There have been guys that I have been working with for thirty years that are not literally blood relatives, but that I would consider close enough. Chicago's known for that. I mean, think of the family bakeries in Chicago. Sure, it's a lot of competition, but they're all great people. They're all really good about things like, our power went out. We need help. Sure, we'll help you. We'll make sure we get that bread out on time. Something about Chicago brings that community together and keeps it together.

While Gonnella waited, he stayed on at the bakery as the sole employee, handling every aspect of the business from mixing and baking to delivery and accounting. Soon, his arranged wife from Italy, Marianna Marcucci, came to Chicago and joined him in the bakery.

In 1896, the Gonnellas moved the bakery over to Sangamon Street. Marianna's brothers—Lawrence, Nicholas and Luigi Marcucci—joined the couple in the early 1900s. Business boomed, and the bakery needed to move to an even larger location. They built a plant and storefront on Erie Street and hired on a fleet of horse-drawn delivery wagons. They were making more than two hundred deliveries a day at that time. McDonnell remembers meeting one of the former drivers of the horse-drawn delivery wagons—his name was Fabio. When she met him, he was 106 years old and told stories of the wagons getting stuck in the snow and having to use the horse to push and pull it out of the drift.

"They used to deliver to homes with the horse and carriage, because there weren't really grocery stores at that time like we know them today," McDonnell said. "There was a dry goods, and there was a fish market and a meat market."

By the end of World War II, wholesale business to grocery stores and restaurants eclipsed home delivery. In the mid-1970s, the bakery entered the frozen dough market, and in 1980, an entire plant in Schaumburg dedicated to frozen dough opened. The Erie Street storefront shop closed in 1994.

Today, Gonnella's production is spread out over five facilities in Illinois and Pennsylvania. The bakeries produce about three million pounds of fresh bread and frozen dough every week. More than thirty family members still work for the company—including McDonnell, whose great-grandfather

Gonnella owners, employees and their families with delivery horses and carriages outside of the Erie Street location in the early 1900s. *Gonnella Baking Company.*

Gonnella's original retail storefront on Erie Street, circa 1950s. *Gonnella Baking Company.*

French bread loaves cooling on a wooden rack. This rack was then rolled into the shipping room to be loaded onto trucks. *Gonnella Baking Company.*

Gonnella driver Hank Davia handing out bread downtown for the company's one hundredth anniversary. The event was a March of Dimes fundraiser. *Gonnella Baking Company.*

was one of the brothers who came over from Italy—in addition to about seven hundred other employees. The board of directors is now on its fourth generation of family leadership.

The employees and their families have always been the heart of the operation at Gonnella.

"There are stories of drivers that weren't sure if they could get into work during snowstorms, so they'd call and somebody else would go pick them up and bring them in," McDonnell said. "We care about families a lot. There are some charities we partner with because they have to do with the families of our employees, they're something that's special to them. It's stuff like that that means a lot to the families of the employees that work here. We support those charities that make a difference in people's lives that work for the company. We really try to care for them as family, and it shows by the longevity in what they do. And they're skilled, really skilled people, especially the bakers. We're really fortunate."

FINGERHUT BAKERY

Multiple Locations

In 1894, Frank Naprstek and his family came to Chicago from Bohemia. When they arrived, they changed their last name. Naprstek means "thimble" in the family's native Czech; *Fingerhut* was just another, more Americanized term for one. Frank was already a fourth-generation baker before he came to the United States. His great-grandfather opened a small bakery in Bohemia in the 1700s and ran it until the 1820s, when he passed it to his son Anthony. Anthony passed it to his son Jan in the mid-1800s, and then Jan passed it to Frank (his son) in the late 1800s. Before coming to the United States, Frank carefully packed all the family recipes into his luggage.

Frank picked a location at 18th and May Streets to continue his family tradition of baking. The first iteration of Fingerhut Home Bakery opened in 1895 and rapidly grew in popularity thanks to old-world kolaches, houska and Babi's rye bread. (Babi is the Czech word for "grandmother," and indeed, Frank used his grandmother's recipe.) In 1921, Frank passed the business on to his son Charles. He moved the bakery to land he bought at Cermak Road and Central Avenue and changed the name of

A 1959 ad for Charles Fingerhut Bakery. *Public domain.*

the business to Charles Fingerhut Bakery. Charles and his family lived above the bakery. By the 1950s, family members owned and operated four different locations in the Chicagoland area. Charles's son, Herb Sr., took over his father's location, and then passed it to his son, Herb Jr. Extended family members eventually opened new Fingerhut locations in Indiana. Those locations—in Knox and North Judson—are still in operation. They are equally historic, with the North Judson location opening in 1946 and the Knox location in 1978.

Fans of the card game canasta may be familiar with canasta cake, a two-layer square chocolate cake with chocolate buttercream filling, frosted with chocolate fudge and trimmed with chocolate sprinkles. Well, we can thank Charles Fingerhut Bakery for that cake. In the 1950s, as canasta the game was sweeping the nation, Charles and Herb wanted to capitalize on it—so they invented the cake to go alongside the game.

In the early 2000s, Fingerhut Bakery closed after 105 years of business—but not before firmly solidifying its spot as a beloved part of the community. Families came in for generations to buy their rye bread and other sweet treats. The bread was so popular that Fingerhut baked 600 pounds daily and 1,200 pounds on the weekends.

Cakes became ever more popular as the bakery and community grew. A former employee remembered that once, a local group was trying to raise money for an injured child. One of the fund raisers asked Fingerhut to donate a small thank-you cake for people who had donated—and when he came back to pick it up, Herb Sr. gave him an elaborate cake to feed two hundred people. The man began to cry and so did every employee and customer in the shop at the time. It was that type of generosity that kept customers coming in year after year.

SCHULZE AND BURCH BISCUIT CO.

1133 West 35th Street in Bridgeport

In 1896, Paul Schulze left Germany for the United States. That same year, he founded the Schulze Baking Company in Garfield Park, at the intersection of Wabash Avenue and Garfield Boulevard. He spent those first years baking bread, a loaf he called Butternut. Schulze Baking Company quickly gained notoriety as one of the largest commercial bread bakeries in the country. Schulze commissioned an architect, John Ahlschlager, to build him a grand early art deco factory—eleven years before the architectural style even gained popularity in Paris. The inside needed to be equipped for an enormous bakery, complete with assembly lines and conveyor ovens.

The factory opened for business in 1914. There was a factory outlet on the corner, and tours ended in free cupcakes. Schulze insisted the building was solving a public health problem running rampant in the United States at the time. In a 1911 speech to the American Bakers' Association (of which he was president), he claimed American housewives were serving their husbands deadly loaves of bread. According to Schulze, home ovens didn't get hot enough to cook bread all the way through and the center ended up raw. He suggested the loaves ended up carrying bacterial disease, and when the wives served it, they were "unquestionably committing murder," he said in his speech. Thankfully, though, the ovens in his bread palace would easily reach the proper temperature, thereby ending the scourge of death by undercooked loaf. *The New York Times* reprinted his claim, and it gave commercial baking operations a healthy economic boost.

Schulze wouldn't get to enjoy his factory for too long. After only seven years, he suffered a head injury and had to retire. Butternut bread stayed in production thanks to the following two owners, Interstate Bakeries and Lewis Bakeries. The factory closed in 2004.

Retirement didn't suit Schulze, and two years after he retired, he was back at work. This time, he and his son, Paul Jr., acquired two small bakeries and formed them into the Paul Schulze Biscuit Company. Their main product? Saltine crackers. In fact, the very first saltines in the world came from the Paul Schulze Biscuit Company, with a trademark to prove it.

In 1939, Paul Schulze Biscuit Company combined with Burch Biscuit Company, which was originally created as a subsidiary of the Schulze brand. The business was renamed the Schulze and Burch Biscuit Company. During World War II, it was tapped by the government to provide all-purpose survival biscuits for fallout shelters and soldier rations. Occasionally, some leftover tins of them are found in fallout shelters or old basements, still labeled with the Schulze and Burch name.

After the war, Schulze and Burch switched to more consumer-based treats. They began to manufacture granola bars and toaster pastries in addition to the crackers. A new 350,000-square-foot factory opened in Bridgeport, where the business still operates today with five hundred employees. The company's Toast'em Pop-Ups are the second-best sellers in the toaster pastry world, falling in line behind Pop-Tarts.

IMPERIAL BAKERY

1011 North Damen Avenue in Ukrainian Village

In its heyday, Imperial Bakery was known for its rye bread—a medium-weight Polish rye with a healthy sprinkling of caraway; a hard, shiny crust; and a tender interior. When the bakery sold to S. Rosen, families who loved the bread were devastated. But what a lot of people don't know is that the bread is still available to buy fresh.

Imperial's founder, Louis Dworkin, came to the United States from Russia in the early 1900s. He was a baker in his homeland, and he continued that tradition in Chicago when he opened the bakery shortly after his arrival. He sold his bread in red, green and white paper wrappers, with a paper tag at the end of every loaf. Dworkin hired local teens to drive delivery trucks, and younger neighborhood kids would come work in the bakery after school. One former "employee" remembers his time at the bakery:

> *My friend and I worked there illegally (we were twelve) "catching buns," kaiser rolls, as they came down the conveyor belt and were dropped into tall paper bags. There was an electric eye counter and one had simply to fold the tall bag closed when the gross (or whatever the count was) had fallen into the bag and clear the occasional "bun jam" on the belt. Tedious—no wonder that the teenage truck drivers whose job this actually was would throw us a couple of bucks so they could go on "smoke break." The line was just off the loading dock, and the bags were immediately shuttled into the dark blue bakery trucks for delivery city-wide.*
>
> *This was incredibly exciting work for a twelve-year-old boy. And at any time, you could just grab a fresh, hot, perfect kaiser roll right off the line*

and eat it. No bread experience since has matched it. I won't bore you with the other escapades of kids let loose in the bakery (fire extinguisher battles, "ice skating" in the walk-in cooler, bun fights, etc.) but those were amazing and formative summer days. Of course, my parents knew nothing about it.

In the 1970s, bakery strikes and labor troubles were rampant, and freshly baked bread became increasingly difficult to find—including Imperial's famed rye. Dworkin sold the operation to S. Rosen in 1976. He did, however, retain the bakery name.

In 1982, Dworkin's son Arnold bought Kaufman's Deli in Skokie. It's owned by his daughter Bette now. Imperial rye devotees will find a pleasant surprise waiting for them at Kaufman's: the original rye bread, baked from the same recipe, branded as Imperial Bakery bread.

SCAFURI BAKERY

1337 West Taylor Street in Little Italy

The history of Scafuri Bakery begins in 1901, when Luigi Scafuri left Calabria, Italy, and came to Chicago. He brought along his wife, Carmella; their first child, Frances; and his father, Giovanni. The family settled in Little Italy, among a tight-knit group of Italian immigrants. Scafuri Bakery opened in 1904 and became immediately successful thanks to its old-world bread and classic Italian pastries. Luigi developed the bakery's menu as a nod to his heritage.

Luigi successfully ran Scafuri Bakery until 1955. Times were sometimes tough, like during the Great Depression. But Luigi used the bakery to help the community through it, giving families free bread on Saturdays. Luigi and Carmella had six more children throughout the time they ran the shop. When he died in 1955, their daughter Annette Mategrano took over the business, running it with her husband, Pasquale, for more than fifty more years. She was ninety when she retired and the bakery closed in 2007.

Luigi's dream of the bakery didn't die when Annette retired, though. In 2010, his great-great-niece Michelle DiGiovanni-Harold revived the shop. She recruited her own niece, Kelly, to help run the bakery and set to updating the building and reestablishing the business. Scafuri Bakery reopened in 2013. Today, longtime customers who've been eating there for generations can come see the historic building with family pictures lining the walls. The menu still speaks to that Calabrian heritage. Some of the favorite items are lemon ricotta pound cake, cannoli, fresh bread, biscotti, cuccidati, bombolini, pignoli and thick Roman-style pizza squares.

W.A. WALLACE BAKERY COMPANY

3634 South State Street in Douglas

When Chicago hosted an exposition in 1915 for the fiftieth anniversary of the emancipation of enslaved people, a prominent baker showed attendees how to make biscuits. That baker was William Alexander Wallace, one of the city's most important Black businessmen of the time. Wallace ran the W.A. Wallace Bakery Company, a retail-turned-wholesale business that sold its bread in more than seventy-five stores around Chicago.

The W.A. Wallace Bakery Company began operations in 1904. Wallace and his wife borrowed twenty-nine dollars to open the first shop. He was working with the postal service in the evenings then, leaving his wife to bake bread and rolls; stock the shelves with the baked goods and some groceries; and run the store with his help as he was able. The bread and rolls took off, and the Wallaces upgraded their oven—first from a kitchen gas stove to a twenty-loaf gas oven and then to an eighty-loaf portable coal oven. Business grew so rapidly that Wallace quit his job with the postal service, bought a delivery wagon and a horse and came to the bakery full time. Soon, they were supplying bread all over the city. In 1906, the Wallaces incorporated the business.

Running a bakery wasn't easy for Wallace. He faced an economic downturn that left him $1,000 in debt; battled with unions and cut-rate bakeries offering the same products for cheaper and worse quality; and faced bouts of racism every day as a successful Black baker in a largely white industry. But the company prevailed, growing ever larger and helping Wallace become more known in the community and around the country. He regularly traveled to conventions and schools in the United States to give speeches and discuss the bakery business.

In 1924, the W.A. Wallace Bakery Company closed its doors. Wallace moved from baking into politics. In 1926, he was the secretary general of the Universal Negro Improvement Association, which is still in operation today. Following that, he worked in the Cook County Recorder's Office. In 1938, he was elected the first Black state senator in Illinois.

VESECKY'S BAKERY

6634 West Cermak Road in Berwyn

No matter when you stop by Vesecky's in Berwyn, you're almost always guaranteed to wait in line—and to hear the longest anyone has ever waited. For the record, the longest published wait time was three hours, just before Easter.

"But what are you going to do? You can't go home empty-handed," the customer told the *Chicago Tribune*.

The food causing those lines is just as legendary. Most customers describe the bakery as the one and only place for traditional Czech baked goods. They're waiting hours for things like poppy seed coffee bread, kolacky, Bohemian rye bread and the bakery's iconic houska, a lightly sweet yeasted bread full of raisins, braided and topped with almonds. The houska is shipped all over the country to customers.

"There used to be a couple of Bohemian bakeries on every block out here but not anymore," third-generation former owner James Vesecky Jr. said. "So many of my customers are senior citizens. When they move, I send to them by mail order. They have to have their houska. Where are they going to get it in Florida?"

Vesecky's is now on the fourth generation, owned by Dave and Randy Vesecky. The bakery has been operating for more than a century. Bohemil and Anna Vesecky opened it in Chicago in 1905, shortly after they immigrated to the United States from Czechoslovakia. They passed the business on to their son James during the Depression, who ran the bakery with his wife, Alice. The couple moved the store from Chicago to 6234 Cermak Road in Berwyn. There, James baked, and Alice ran the store and managed the staff. In the 1960s, they moved locations again, to the current spot at 6634 Cermak Road. James and Alice eventually passed the business to their son, James Jr., who then passed it to sons Dave and Randy in 1995.

FERRARA BAKERY

2210 West Taylor Street in Tri-Taylor

In 1900, Salvatore Ferrara emigrated from Italy to New York. He had spent years in Italy studying in the seminary to become a priest, when suddenly his father died. He instantly became the head of the family, taking care of four siblings and his mother. But they were running out of money. So he and his family agreed he would come to the United States to work. An extended family member who owned a restaurant sponsored his trip to New York, and Ferrara went to work in the kitchen there.

"He spent a year living in the kitchen of that restaurant in New York," said Nella Davy, Ferrara's granddaughter and the current owner of Ferrara Bakery. "He slept there for a year, just to pay back the money for the boat ride."

Ferrara continued his studies in that kitchen, reading books in the evening. After he paid off his debt, he took that knowledge to Texas, where he served as an interpreter between Italian laborers working on the railroad and their foreman. He saved all the money he made on that job, and in 1908, he moved to Chicago and opened Ferrara Bakery at 772 West Taylor Street. His family in Italy had a baking background, making cakes, cookies, pastries and confetti (or, as many people know them, Jordan almonds). Ferrara Bakery continued that tradition as the first Italian pastry shop in Chicago.

In the early days, Ferrara joined forces with his brother, John Ferrara, and Salvatore Lezza (his sister's husband). Then, in 1918, he married Serafina Pagano, another Italian immigrant who came over to Chicago when she was just nine years old and spoke no English. At that time, the candy business was taking off—the company is known for Jordan almonds and some national favorite candies like Lemonheads, Fireballs and Red Hots—and he couldn't keep up. So he separated into two companies in 1920: Ferrara Bakery and Ferrara Pan Candy Company. He built a new facility at 2210 West Taylor Street to manufacture candy. In 1922, Serafina took over the bakery with her two brothers, and John Ferrara and Lezza left the business.

Ferrara Bakery quickly became known for its massive wedding cakes, with the cannoli cake being the most popular flavor. It has three layers of cake and two layers of filling: one layer is cannoli cream and the other layer is fresh strawberries with custard. (They still make the cake today.) And the wedding cakes were huge, feeding up to one thousand people. In fact, in 1931, Ferrara Bakery won a gold medal and earned a record for baking the world's biggest cake. It weighed 2,000 pounds. Another cake weighed 375 pounds and fed one thousand people; that one was made for Dominic Marchese and Edith Gentile's wedding around the 1950s. It was an arch cake, meaning the couple could stand under an arch made entirely of cake. The flavor was rum-soaked sponge with pineapple and custard filling, topped with marshmallow meringue. And the topper was eight white plastic slippers and a wedding ornament. Baker Mario Conti, a twenty-eight-year-old army

Above: Ferrara Bakery's original storefront at 772 West Taylor Street in 1918. *From left to right*: Salvatore Lezza, John Ferrara and Salvatore Ferrara. *Ferrara Bakery.*

Left: Ferrara Bakery's current storefront. *Author's collection.*

veteran at the time, made the cake and decorated it by hand. Some of the wedding cakes were so tall that Serafina needed to climb a ladder just to get to the top layer and start cutting. And others had live doves in them; there was a cage three or four layers down from the top, and the doves would fly out when the cage was opened. It was considered good luck.

Opposite: Gene and Theresa (Curro) Skika pose under their Ferrara Bakery wedding cake on September 23, 1949. *Ferrara Bakery.*

Left: Serafina Ferrara climbs up behind a table to reach the top of a wedding cake. *Ferrara Bakery.*

"The cake was a focal point in Italian weddings," Davy said. "It was a really big deal."

The cakes were part of a larger tradition called peanut weddings, Davy said. They had the cake, peanuts in the shell, beef sandwiches and, if it was a Ferrara Bakery wedding, they'd also have confetti (Jordan almonds). Peanut weddings are a Chicago-specific term for the tradition, which dates back to the early 1900s, when new Italian immigrants had so little money that they could only afford to have peanuts at their weddings. As future generations gained more wealth, the term stuck, but the food selection expanded.

In 1955, Serafina launched a new business because of those weddings. Prior to that date, weddings were always held in church basements, in a hotel or in a labor union hall. So that year, Serafina kicked off the wedding reception trade. She opened the very first catering hall in the city of Chicago, at Chicago Avenue and Central, called Chateau Royale. It was in a former theater, and 1,500 people could fit upstairs, 500 downstairs. She decorated it in an opulent style, with sculptures and chandeliers. Everything was imported from Italy so it would have an old-world feel. She soon opened a second one at North and Central, called Ferrara Manor, and then other

A Ferrara Bakery cake made to look like the ship *Emanuel* in 1919. *Ferrara Bakery.*

Mayor Richard J. Daley (*far right*) and Serafina Ferrara (*on his left*) celebrating Chicago's birthday on March 4, 1960. *Ferrara Bakery.*

POST CARD

PLA
2 CENT
STAMP
HERE

"REMEMBER," your guests at the next party will be greatly delighted if you serve them with some sweets put up by the

'Original' Pasticceria Ferrara & Co.
722 W. Taylor Street
CHICAGO, ILL.
TEL. MONROE 2201

We hold the world's record for having put up the largest and most elaborate Wedding Cake.

Office and Factory at 2200-10 West
treet.

A postcard depicting Serafina Ferrara and her brother James Pagano in 1925 at 722 West Taylor Street. *Ferrara Bakery.*

> Nella Davy on the Serendipity of Wedding Cakes
>
> I had a wedding cake this weekend for an older woman. She wanted Italian, and she called and made an order with my son. Then she talked to her sister, who asked where she'd gotten her wedding cake. She told her sister Ferrara's. And her sister said, "That's where I got my cake from thirty years ago! And that's where Mom got hers sixty-five years ago!" She couldn't believe it. She got the same cake as her sister and her mother and didn't even know it.

companies caught on and opened their own. Chicago locals will know names like Drury Lane and Condesa Del Mar—they learned from Serafina.

"Her vision, for a woman who came here at age nine with no education, was incredible," Davy said.

Serafina was really the star of the bakery—and of the entire community at the time. If families needed food, she gave it to them. If kids needed a job to stay off the streets in the summer, she invented one for them. She held Christmas parties, complete with a Santa and gifts, for impoverished children. She helped employees with down payments on homes. She helped build a halfway house for the homeless and a retirement home for Italian seniors. She attended every wake on the near west side to console people, even if she didn't know them. It got to the point where local funeral homes always had a chair reserved for her. She did so much good in the community that she earned the nickname the Angel of Halsted Street. By the time she died in 1975, she was godmother to about two hundred people—all children of families that she helped.

In the mid-1950s, the candy factory moved to a bigger location in Forest Park. The building sat empty until 1963, when the University of Illinois at Chicago came in and razed the entire neighborhood the bakery was in. The bakery moved into the candy factory building, where it remains today, producing all the recipes exactly the same as when Ferrara first started the business.

LEONARD'S BAKERY

2151 West Devon Avenue in West Rogers Park

When Marc Becker took over Leonard's Bakery from his father, it was already on its fifth generation of ownership. The Jewish bakery first opened in 1908 on the southwest side of the city. Becker's grandparents Joe and Dora ran the shop under the name Joe Becker's Bakery. Their son, Leonard, worked there his entire life, learning the secrets of the bakery trade from his parents.

"As young as seven years old, his father would ask him to come downstairs and make a dough with him," Bonnie Stern, Leonard's daughter, said when her father turned one hundred in 2018. "Being a kosher bakery, at that time, besides challah and breads, they only made kichel, mandel bread, sponge, honey and pound cakes."

Leonard took over in the 1950s, after spending three years in the army as a staff (mess) sergeant, from 1943 to 1946, and getting married. He renamed the shop Leonard's Bakery and quickly moved it north to the thriving Jewish community on Devon Avenue.

"After bringing the bakery to Devon Avenue, my dad had wonderful bakers and continued to work at anything that needed to be done, including making his own deliveries," Stern said in 2018. "Some of his favorite things, beside his wonderful twisted challah, are a type of rugelach he called straw and sawdust, chocolate chip coffee cake and a Zadie (grandfather) cookie named after his father, which is doused in cinnamon."

Leonard, his wife, and their four children all lived above the bakery. Leonard baked while his wife managed the store. In 1987, the couple retired to Florida and Marc took over. He moved the shop to suburban Northbrook, where it remained until Marc retired in 2020.

Leonard's Bakery devotees don't have to completely give up the baked goods they once loved. The business was purchased by the Once Upon family of restaurants on the north shore, and it continues to produce Marc's coffeecakes, kiddush cakes, rugelach and more.

LEZZA SPUMONI AND DESSERTS

4009 St. Charles Road in Bellwood

Although Lezza Spumoni and Desserts is out in Bellwood now, the first sixty years of its existence were in Little Italy. It was first a partnership with another longstanding bakery in Chicago, Ferrara Bakery. Salvatore Lezza immigrated to the United States from Naples in 1905, carrying along a secret spumoni recipe. He had plans to open a shop with that recipe. Once in Chicago, he met Salvatore Ferrara, who had come to the city from Italy five years before Lezza. The two joined forces, and in 1908, they opened Chicago's first Italian bakery, Ferrara-Lezza and Co., at 772 West Taylor Street. Local Italian immigrants found what they'd been missing from home in that bakery, and pastries, wedding cakes and confections pushed business through the roof.

Eventually the companies split, and Salvatore passed the business down to his sons, Victor Sr. and Jack. Under their leadership, Lezza continued producing spumoni and a line of baked goods. The spumoni was by far the most popular product, even being featured in the Italian Pavilion at the 1933 World's Fair in Chicago. Lezza sold about 500,000 pounds of it every year. It's made with four layers of ice cream—chocolate, strawberry, rum and pistachio—surrounding a whipped cream core that's mixed with candied fruit and bits of wheat germ.

In the 1960s, the University of Illinois at Chicago moved into the neighborhood, displacing many of the local Italian immigrants and their businesses. The Lezza's property was deemed condemned, and the business was forced to relocate to Bellwood. Eventually, Lezza opened a café in Elmhurst as well. As of this writing, the company is on its fourth generation of ownership.

POMPEI

1531 West Taylor Street in Little Italy

Alphonso Davino never wanted to be a baker. But one night when he was eighteen, one of the bakers at Pompei, Davino's father's bakery, didn't show up. Davino hopped onto the line to make bread, and nothing was ever the same. He fell in love with baking and, after his dad retired, went on to run the bakery for thirty years. Pompei is still in operation today.

Luigi Davino (Alphonso's father) opened Pompei at 818 South Loomis Street in 1909. He didn't name it after the famous archaeological site, though; he named it in honor of the local church, Our Lady of Pompeii. Luigi; his wife, Carmella; their four sons; and their daughter all lived above the bakery.

In the early years, the bakery sold only bread and cheese pizza, cooking with a hand-me-down oven built in 1890. Luigi did his best to

Alphonso Davino on the Decline of Little Italy

The neighborhood on Taylor Street used to be like the old country. All the traditions, all the food. You walked down the street and you could smell the wine being made in peoples' homes. It was like a big family. Everybody was connected in some way, not maybe through bloodlines, but it was pretty close. The neighborhood started to change when the medical centers and students moved in. By the 1970s, the younger generations of the families were starting to drift apart. At one time, the city of Chicago had 735 Italian bakeries. By 1970, there were only 19 left, and most of them had stopped making bread and started making pastries and cakes. We never made cakes and sweets.

adapt to the times during his ownership of Pompei. During the Depression, he cut bread prices to two cents a pound just to ensure the bakery stayed open, keeping his family's livelihood intact. All four of his sons—Alphonso, Ralph, Salvatore and Roger—were eventually drafted in World War II.

"I worked hard to build up the bakery, especially when my boys went in the army," Luigi once said. "Back then, you had to have two things, a strong back and a strong will to survive."

When the boys returned from the war, Alphonso took control of the bakery. He carried on his father's schedule of baking bread in the morning, having every loaf out of the oven by 11:30 a.m. and wrapping it only once it was sold. His brothers worked at Pompei with him. Another baker, Giuseppe Esposito, an Italian immigrant, helped out on Saturdays. Esposito never put bread in the oven or took it out, though. Each loaf weighed two and a half pounds, and about 320 loaves went into the oven at one time; Esposito couldn't handle the weight.

Alphonso continued baking bread at Pompei until his retirement in the 1980s. The entire time, he followed old-world methods and recipes. "Everybody in the old country makes bread the same way," he explained, calling out the only ingredients: flour, salt, water and yeast. He also refused to move to a more commercial baking operation, not wanting to replace that personal touch.

"I like to make the bread because it makes me feel good to make something genuine," he said in 1977. "Each loaf has a character of its own. Commercial bread is cold. It all looks alike. When the finished product comes out of the oven [at my bakery], you know you accomplished something."

That bread recipe, now more than one hundred years old, is still used at the bakery. After Alphonso retired, his nephew Ralph took over the

Above: Alphonso Davino's father, the founder of Pompei, in a photo taken in the 1930s. *Library of Congress.*

Left: Alphonso Davino displays finished bread inside Pompei. *Library of Congress.*

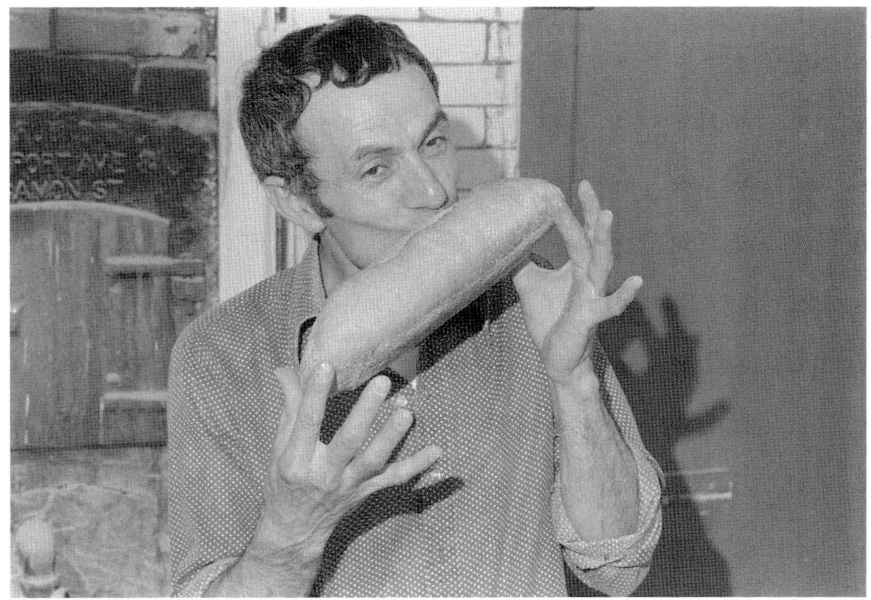

Baker Giuseppe Esposito poses with Italian bread at Pompei. *Library of Congress.*

Bakers Alphonso Davino, Roger Davino and Guiseppe Esposito shape dough into loaves. *Library of Congress.*

Alphonso Davino removing loaves from the oven at Pompei. *Library of Congress.*

business. Pompei has moved several times, expanded twice, endured a family lawsuit about multiple locations using the same name and finally settled into its current location on Taylor Street. The bakery is on its fourth generation of ownership and sells a robust selection of Italian specialties, including pasta, calamari and pizza strudel. According to Ralph, Pompei debuted the fast-casual dining style in the 1980s, pioneering the era of people ordering at a counter and having food brought to their tables. Alphonso died in 1987.

ALPHA BAKING COMPANY

Multiple Locations

There's a constant battle in Chicago, one that divides family and friends (in tastes at least): Do you prefer your rye bread seeded or unseeded? Well, Alpha Baking has the ultimate answer. By a thin margin, customers prefer seeded rye bread. At least that's what the sales figures of S. Rosen's bread show.

S. Rosen's (later part of the Alpha Baking family) got its start in 1909. The founder, Sam Rosen, came over from Poland in 1886, when he was just thirteen years old. He'd been training as a baker since he was nine, and by the time he came to the United States, he was already a certified master baker. He first went to New York and opened his own bakery when he turned sixteen. He specialized in rye bread. In New York, Rosen helped organize the first baker's union in the city and led a strike, advocating for bakers to get a twelve-hour day, a six-day week and twelve dollars a week in pay. The strike was successful but left Rosen with an injury; he was hit over the head by a strikebreaker and lost hearing in one ear as a result.

In his early twenties, Rosen moved to Chicago. He bought a small bakery, the New York Baking Company, on the northwest side. He renamed it to S. Rosen's and sold the rye bread that made his bakery famous in New York. He delivered it by horse-drawn wagon, unwrapped and put into breadboxes that were set outside grocery stores in the city. In 1961, Sam retired, and his son Don took over. Don's son, Steve, joined the company in 1974. Steve is still working at Alpha Baking today, as are his children. Now, though, deliveries are made by electric truck.

Signs at the Alpha Baking Company's Polk Street facility. *Alpha Baking Company.*

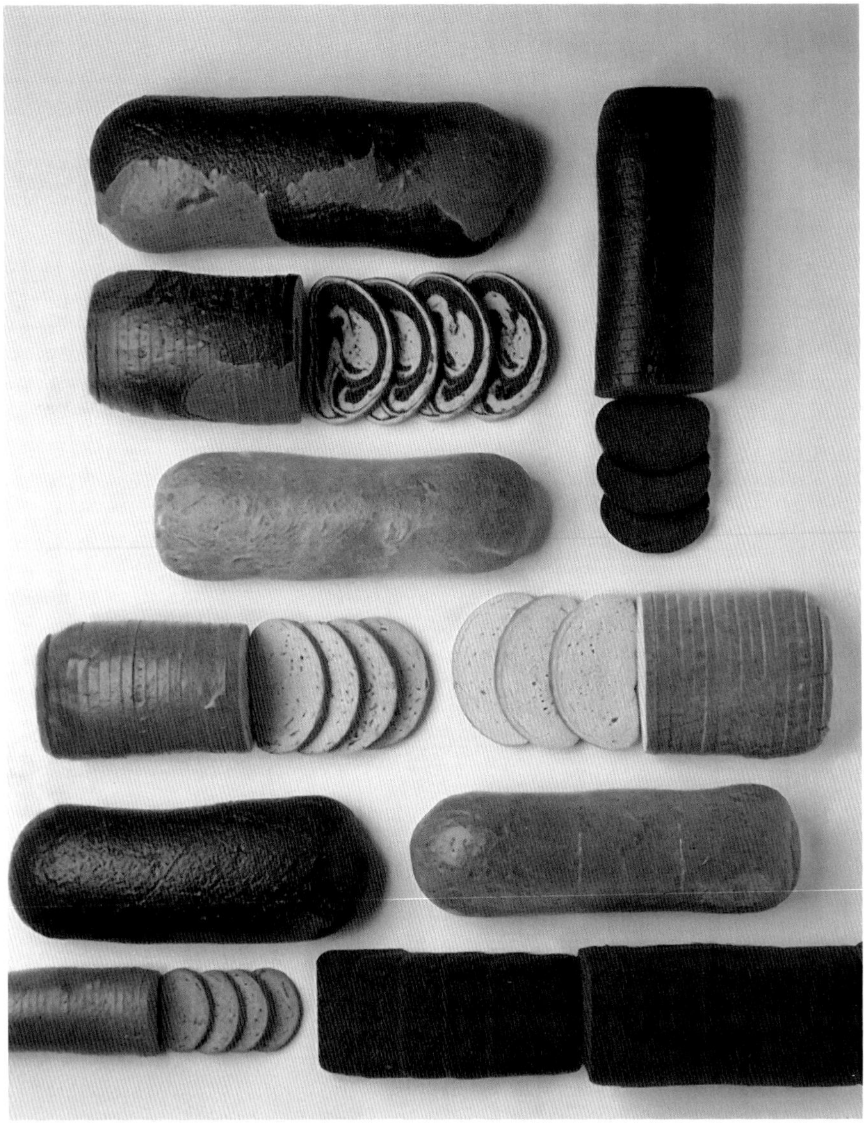

Alpha Baking Company produces a wide variety of bread styles. *Alpha Baking Company.*

As S. Rosen's was growing, so was Mary Ann Bakery (now also part of the Alpha Baking family). Owner Louis Kuchuris bought the already-existing shop when he was twenty-six years old. The bakery was known for bread, rolls, pastries and buns, and it was one of the largest wholesale bakeries in the Midwest, servicing 1,800 businesses. In 1955, Mary Ann

Burger buns on the line at Alpha Baking Company's Lyndale Avenue bakery. *Author's collection.*

Bakery became the first official bun supplier for McDonald's in suburban Des Plaines. Within fifteen years, Mary Ann was providing buns for forty McDonald's stores in the area. Fast food aside, the bakery became famous for its poppy seed hot dog bun, an essential ingredient of the iconic Chicago-style hot dog.

The stories of S. Rosen's and Mary Ann collide in 1981. Alpha Baking Company purchased Mary Ann Bakery from Kuchuris in 1979, and in 1981, it acquired S. Rosen's (including all the family members in the business). A few more bakeries have been purchased over the years, all under the Alpha Baking umbrella. Mary Ann Bakery had previously operated out of a facility at 4545 West Lyndale Avenue, and Alpha Baking kept that facility for hamburger and hot dog bun production. The products are co-branded as S. Rosen's and Mary Ann. The building is now more than one hundred years old, with visible antique wooden high beams in the shipping dock. Alpha Baking's corporate headquarters is now on Polk Street, and there's a sweet goods facility in what was once the original Sara Lee plant.

The S. Rosen's and Mary Ann products are iconic in Chicago. The rye bread is still made with Sam Rosen's original rye starter, making it more than one hundred years old and still going strong. It's kept in a special mixer in the

Left: Wooden beams from the original building at Alpha Baking Company's Lyndale Avenue bakery are visible in the shipping dock. *Author's collection.*

Below: Pullman loaves from Mary Ann Bakery were designed to easily stack into Pullman train cars. *Author's collection.*

Shirts from the 2019 Chicago Hot Dog Fest. *Alpha Baking Company.*

bakery. During the summer, more than one million poppy seed buns come off the line, supplying 95 percent of the hot dog stands in Chicago. Stephanie Powell, director of marketing at Alpha Baking, says it's the authenticity and longevity of the products that keep them popular.

"It's the mark that you actually cared, and that you actually cared about Chicago's history," Powell said. "You have people from outside of Chicago come in, and they don't realize how significant a Chicago hot dog is. It's all the cultures of Chicago mashing up, and to leave out one part of it is leaving out part of Chicago's history. So, it's the mark of authenticity."

Plus, says Michael Thornburg, plant manager for Alpha Baking, the food is just superior. Nothing stands up to hefty Chicago food like S. Rosen's. Particularly for Chicago dogs, the hinge strength on the bun is exemplary.

"It's something that outside of being a baker, a lot of people probably won't consider too much," Thornburg said. "Going into what keeps the hot dog held together, really, it's that hinge on the end after you've sliced it. Because of its longevity, you don't have to eat the hot dog immediately after the bread was sliced."

The poppy seed hot dog buns have been part of some major Chicago events. In 2004, during the Taste of Chicago, S. Rosen's set a world record for the largest bun; it was 37.2 feet long and covered in poppy seeds. And in 2005,

S. Rosen's hot dog buns come off the packaging line on antique equipment still in use at the bakery on Lyndale Avenue. *Author's collection.*

A sign for S. Rosen's dark rye bread. *Alpha Baking Company.*

S. Rosen's partnered with Vienna Beef to sign a "Piece Treaty." The two company presidents at the time, Howard Eirinberg from Vienna Beef and Mark Marcucci at Alpha Baking, spent a year trying to resolve the enduring problem of hot dogs being sold in packages of eight and buns being sold in packages of six or twelve. Eirinberg found that because of the mismatch, about two million buns were going to waste every year. The two CEOs signed an actual treaty document, and S. Rosen's began selling buns in packages of eight. After signing, they went downtown to the Thompson Center and gave away about one thousand hot dogs for one-dollar donations to the Greater Chicago Food Depository.

S. Rosen's famous rye bread doesn't escape the Chicago stunts, either. Back around the 1950s, the Harlem Globetrotters were putting on regular shows in the city. Attendees said the team was so skilled with their ball handling that the only thing they couldn't do with a basketball was eat it. The Globetrotters took that as a challenge and enlisted S. Rosen's bakers to create a basketball they could eat. The eventual product was a bread-covered basketball that matched the color of the actual basketballs. It looked like a real basketball from a distance, but they shocked the crowd when, mid-pass, the players stopped to take a bite from it.

That interaction with the community has always been important to S. Rosen's, Mary Ann and Alpha Baking overall. The company sponsors Little League teams; donates food heavily to the city, including to the police department, the fire department and churches; and uses electric trucks to be quieter around neighbors and pollute less.

"I'm fourth or fifth-generation Chicagoan," Powell said. "It's kind of cool when you have a long involvement in Chicago food history. It's important not to forget that it matters to a place. In a time when you have these big corporations that are completely detached, you have a family-run business that's still making something super-traditional. It's an honor to be part of something that helps a place be unique."

FROM THE ALPHA BAKING RECIPE BOX

Chicago-Style Hot Dog

A Chicago-style hot dog has to start with an S. Rosen's Mary Ann poppy seed hot dog bun. It's the mark of a true Chicago-style dog and has been since this culinary creation emerged from Maxwell Street in the 1930s.

Ingredients

1 all-beef hot dog, prepared in your style of choice
1 S. Rosen's Mary Ann poppy seed hot dog bun
Yellow mustard, to taste
Neon green relish, to taste
Diced white onion, to taste
1 Roma tomato slice, cut in half
1 dill pickle spear
2 sport peppers
Dash celery salt

Directions

Start by placing hot dog into bun. Then add mustard to one side of bun. Next add neon green relish, diced onion, tomato, pickle, sport peppers and celery salt.

Classic Reuben Sandwich

The classics never go out of style. Enjoy this simple recipe for a delicious Reuben sandwich that's sure to make your mouth water. It's perfect for St. Patrick's Day, but so tasty, we suspect you'll want to have it more than just once a year. Our tip: Bring out your meat and cheese 20 to 30 minutes before you create your sandwiches for a better result.

Ingredients

2 tablespoons Thousand Island dressing
2 slices S. Rosen's rye bread
¼ pound thinly sliced deli corned beef
2 slices Swiss cheese
2 to 4 ounces sauerkraut, drained
Butter

Directions

Spread about 1 tablespoon of Thousand Island dressing over each slice of rye bread. Build your sandwich with corned beef, Swiss cheese and sauerkraut. Top with remaining bread slice.

Heat a generous dollop of butter in a pan (cast iron works best). Cook sandwich uncovered on medium heat for about 4 minutes, or until golden brown. Add more butter if needed before flipping

Flip your sandwich and cook for another 3 minutes, or until golden brown. Transfer to your plate and enjoy.

BBQ-Style Corned Beef, Guinness BBQ Sauce, Honey Mustard Slaw and Pepper Jack Cheese

This preparation takes corned beef and rye in a whole different direction—barbeque! We created a smoky and sweet BBQ sauce using Guinness and a crunchy slaw to make this unique creation. Both the BBQ sauce and coleslaw can be made in advance for ease of serving.

Guinness BBQ Sauce

½ cup ketchup
⅓ cup molasses
⅓ cup apple cider vinegar
1 teaspoon mustard powder
1 teaspoon powdered ginger
5 teaspoons smoked paprika
1 teaspoon garlic powder
1 ½ teaspoons salt

¼ teaspoon chipotle powder
⅛ teaspoon cinnamon
1 12-ounce bottle of Guinness Draught
1 tablespoon brown sugar

Assemble all ingredients, except the Guinness and brown sugar, in a bowl.

Pour Guinness in a medium-high preheated pan. Once it starts to bubble, add the brown sugar. Simmer for 5 minutes at medium-high heat.

Add the rest of the ingredients, bring to the beginning of a simmer, then reduce heat to medium and simmer gently for 20 minutes.

Honey Mustard Cabbage Slaw

½ cup mayonnaise
2 teaspoons salt
1 tablespoon mustard
2 tablespoons honey
2 tablespoons apple cider vinegar
½ teaspoon paprika
½ teaspoon garlic powder
1 head of cabbage, sliced into thin ribbons

Whisk together all ingredients except cabbage until smooth. Add sliced cabbage into mixture and stir to combine.

BBQ-Style Corned Beef Sandwich

2 slices S. Rosen's rye bread
4 ounces corned beef
2 slices pepper jack cheese

Preheat oven to 350.

For each sandwich, place 2 rye bread slices on baking sheet. Top one with corned beef, brush with Guinness BBQ sauce and top with pepper jack cheese. Bake for 7 minutes or until cheese is melted.

To serve, top with coleslaw and second slice of rye bread.

BURNY BROTHERS BAKERY

Multiple Locations

Remember this?

Who are we?
Burny Brothers!
Bakers who are partic-tic-ticular
Because of you!
We never stop baking, day or night,
We never stop baking, day or night!

If you don't remember the jingle, you might remember Burny Brothers' products: butter bread, lebkuchen, egg bread, Louisiana crunch cake, brownies, French crumb cake, cinnamon streusel coffeecake, sugar cookies and graham cracker cake with whipped cream. If you didn't buy them in the early days of the bakery, you bought them at the grocery store or at Wrigley Field. Or maybe you just remember the delivery trucks with "Burny Bros. Better Bread" written on the side.

Burny Brothers Bakery opened in 1910, founded by three French immigrants: C.J., Jule and George Burny. They were coal miners before starting the bakery, and fellow miners told them it would never work out. But the Burny brothers proved them wrong, growing their business—first called Original French Bakery, at 841 Racine Avenue—into the largest variety baker in the country. By 1950, they had forty wholesale routes and twenty-five retail outlets.

Though the Burny brothers were French, they were taught to bake by a Belgian, Joseph Dutz. He came to the United States to bake at the World's Columbian Exposition in 1893. His wife, Angela, was friends with the Burny family, who were still in Europe. When the boys' father died, their mother worried for their future. She made a deal with Dutz that if the brothers came to the United States, he would teach them to bake. And he did, while the brothers were working in the mine. After Dutz taught them all his recipes, he sold the Burny brothers his bakery in 1910, thus launching the business.

Employees working at Burny overwhelmingly loved their jobs. Many met their future spouses there, and some loved their time at the company so much that it was featured in their obituaries, touting multiple decades of employ. On the company's fiftieth anniversary in 1960, the 1,900 employees threw a celebration dinner for C.J., George and the then-late Jule's widow. All three were presented with commemorative plaques. The owners then quickly turned to acknowledging and honoring the thirty-four employees who had worked there more than twenty-five years. The two longest were Walter Schreier at forty-two years of employ and Margaret Butler at thirty-four years. Memories from employees and their families are regularly shared on Facebook and message boards. One member of the Burny family remembered visiting the factory when they were little and getting bundles of leftover bread dough to play with, which would always escalate into dough wars in their garage. One employee's son remembered his father sharing stories of how he had to drive a horse-drawn wagon to make deliveries during the war years when gas was scarce.

In 1963, Burny Brothers was sold to Beatrice Foods. Beatrice Foods sold off the wholesale division in 1976 and then sold the retail division and all remaining assets to Entenmann's Bakery in 1979. Entenmann's then took the Burny Brothers line off the market, tying the knot on a successful business history of about seventy years.

ERGO'S SWEDISH HOME BAKERY

11239 South Michigan Avenue in Roseland

From 1911 to about 1970, the Ergo family ran a Swedish bakery in Roseland. It was first operated by Axle Ergo and then passed on to John Ergo and his wife, Margaret. In the 1930s, the family had shops on both Michigan Avenue and on Broadway. Locals particularly enjoyed the Boston cream pie at Ergo's.

On January 16, 1971, after the bakery had been out of business for a short time, the building on Michigan Avenue burned down—destroying all the bakery equipment inside that the Ergos still owned. It was about $20,000 worth of damage. That building had a fraught history before the fire and before the Ergos ever took over. It was the family bakery of Eliot Ness, the FBI agent who caught Al Capone. It was Norwegian then, run by Ness's parents, Peter and Emma.

ROESER'S BAKERY

3216 West North Avenue in Humboldt Park

Ask any Chicagoan who knows their bakeries what the oldest operating bakery in the city is, and they'll almost certainly tell you Roeser's Bakery. That fact, though, is up for debate. There's a friendly competition between Roeser's and Ferrara Bakery for who's *actually* the oldest. Roeser's opened in 1911 and has remained in the same spot. Ferrara opened in 1908, but it has changed locations. Furthermore, Roeser's founder, John Roeser Sr., actually started baking in Chicago in 1907 when he opened a wholesale bakery downtown. Plus, the owner of Ferrara points out that theirs is a pastry shop and Roeser's is a bakery. Besides, if we're including bread, the "oldest" honor goes to Gonnella and S. Rosen's, and Scafuri and Pompei are both older than Roeser's. So saying Roeser's is the oldest depends on a couple things. Are we talking baking history in general? Do we mean the oldest continually owned family bakery in the same spot as when it opened? Are we whittling down to pastry versus bakery? That decision is up to you.

Roeser's Bakery might never have opened to begin with, though, if it weren't for a friend of the founder. John Roeser Sr. had planned to immigrate to Australia from Germany, rather than heading to the United States. But a friend convinced him Chicago was the place to be, so they boarded a ship and arrived in 1905. Two years after he arrived, he started a wholesale business with another friend. They were popular, with two horse-drawn wagons for deliveries. But Roeser eventually decided he didn't like the business and branched out onto his own, opening his Humboldt Park shop in 1911, where it's been ever since. Roeser's son John Jr. took over in 1936, his son John III took over in 1976 and the current owner, John IV, took over in 2016.

The Roeser's Bakery sign, still functional and in use at the original location today. *Roeser's Bakery.*

Today, almost all of the recipes are the same as they were when the bakery first opened. Customers have been coming for generations for homemade ice cream, cakes, cookies, donuts, pies and eventually pączki,

John Roeser Sr. with two bakers in the production area about 1913. *Roeser's Bakery.*

The Roeser's Bakery team stands behind the bakery's showcase. *Roeser's Bakery.*

John Roeser stands next to a mixer in the bakery. *Roeser's Bakery.*

Polish sweet yeast dough pastries stuffed with filling. One of the long-lasting bestsellers, John IV says, is the butter loaf, an all-butter braided Danish dough baked in a bread loaf, topped with streusel and sweet roll icing and cut into slices. The bakery is also famous for its complicated-to-bake hot-milk yellow sponge cake with fresh strawberry filling. But above all, Roeser's is known for meeting its customers' needs.

"I'm kind of a yes man," John IV said. "I have a tough time saying no. So, even if it's something that we're not making at the time, I'll look up the formula, and I'll make it for them. Or if it's something new that they're looking to do, that we've never even made, I would be happy to run a test mix and see how it comes out. I don't let them place the order until I run a test mix, though, because I don't want to bank on that test mix. If it doesn't turn out and I'm giving them a bad product, that's not helping anybody. But I think that also has lent very nicely to our longevity, because we are so accommodating and we go above and beyond to satisfy customer needs and make them happy."

To that end, the Roesers once opened a party store next to the bakery called Roeser's Party Palace. People bought their bakery treats and then headed to the store for plates, silverware and party decorations. The store didn't stay profitable, though, so it was converted to apartments.

> John Roeser IV on the Competition Between Historic Chicago Bakeries
>
> There is no competition. We actually all try to band together to bolster each other up, to make each other better. Because honestly, our real competition is the grocery stores of the world, the grocery stores that have the in-store bakeries now that are making all these products in commissaries and freezing them. And then, they're trying to sell month-old product that has a bunch of preservatives in it. We're just trying to make sure, as small mom-and-pop retail bakeries, that people understand that that's not how a baked good is supposed to be. We make all of our fillings from scratch. We educate customers on the importance of and the difference in fresh-made products from scratch, with all-natural ingredients. So the family bakeries, we are not competition. We all work together to make sure that people are coming to us instead of grocery stores. I don't think we are a very fierce breed of people, us bakers. We're not clawing at each other. It's not really a cutthroat business. There's a decent-sized pie, and we're all trying to get a piece.

Roeser's Bakery is also fairly well known thanks to television shows. John III was on several Food Network and TLC cooking competition shows as an assistant; the chef jackets from the events are framed and up in the shop.

"It was funny, one of the competitions he did, they were using one of those little handheld electric saws, and he cut his finger a little bit," John IV said of his father. "And they made the biggest spectacle of it. He was so humiliated and embarrassed, because he was like, no, I'm just going to wrap it and keep working. He certainly wasn't seriously injured. It was just blood. They televised it and made a whole deal with the ambulance pulling up. And in reality, he got driven to the hospital by a producer in a Toyota Camry. He didn't go in an ambulance."

In the future, John IV hopes to pass the bakery to his son, John V, who's currently a toddler. But he won't push it if the youngest John is not interested in the business.

"There's a certain sense of pride, tradition and love that goes into this, and if it's not kept in the family, that love and pride and tradition is lost," John IV said. "But this is not a normal occupation. There's definitely a lot of things to consider and a lot of things to make 100 percent sure you're committed to before diving into this. Would I like him to carry it on? Yeah, absolutely, if it makes him happy, no doubt about it. But at the same time, if he wants to do something else, I'm completely fine with the tradition stopping here, you know? I mean, I've already mapped this out. At that time, if I don't have a successor, we'd have been in business for 140 years. If we close after 140 years… that's a good run."

FROM ROESER'S RECIPE BOX

Chocolate Chip Cookies

Yield: About 48 cookies

Ingredients

12 ounces sugar
12 ounces brown sugar
¼ ounce salt
8 ounces butter
8 ounces all-purpose shortening
8 ounces eggs
¼ ounce vanilla
1 ½ pounds cake flour
1 ½ pounds small bittersweet chocolate chips
.13 ounce baking soda

Directions

On lowest speed with a paddle, cream the sugar, brown sugar, salt, butter and shortening until incorporated and softened. Scrape the bowl. The more you cream these together, the more the cookies will spread because the dough will be softer.

Add the eggs and vanilla slowly, scrape again after fully incorporated. Add the flour, chocolate chips and baking soda. Mix only until the flour is fully incorporated into the dough. Do not over mix.

Scoop the cookies onto parchment paper at 1.5 ounces per cookie. Bake at 400 for 16 minutes or until you see the edges become golden-brown.

Brownies

Yield: About 24 brownies

Ingredients

1 pound plus 4 ounces sugar
8 ounces all-purpose shortening
4 ounces cocoa
¼ ounce salt
8 ounces eggs
2 ounces honey
8½ ounces cake flour
10 ounces pecans, chopped into small pieces
8 ounces milk
3 ounces prepared chocolate devil's food cake batter

Directions

On lowest speed with a paddle, cream the sugar, shortening, cocoa and salt until incorporated and softened. Scrape the bowl.

Add the eggs and honey until incorporated. Scrape again. Add the cake flour and pecans, mixing only until the flour is incorporated. Add the milk and cake batter and mix until incorporated. Do not over mix. The more you mix, the more cake-like your brownie will be. If you like a cake-like brownie, mix away. If you like a denser brownie, mix as little as possible in all these steps.

Bake at 375 for 25 minutes or until you can stick a knife in the middle and pull it out clean.

DRESSEL'S BAKERY

3254 South Wallace Street in Bridgeport

Most Chicagoans recognize the Dressel's name from the freezer section of local grocery stores, but the bakery actually had a storefront in Bridgeport before the commercial business took off. Brothers William, Joseph and Herman Dressel came to the United States in the early 1900s. They settled in suburban Barrington and began to farm. Shortly after that, William and Joseph (teens at the time) moved to Chicago to work in their uncle Lorenz Nock's bakery. They were still teenagers when they bought the bakery from him in 1913. Herman was still too young, but ten years later, in 1923, he joined the team as a partner in the business.

Herman was the creative one of the bunch, and in the early 1920s, he suggested a product that would become the bakery's bestseller: a chocolate fudge whipped cream cake. The cake is split into three sections—a chocolate fudge cake on the bottom, then a full inch of whipped cream filling, then another layer of chocolate fudge cake. All the layers are the exact same height. The entire thing is covered in chocolate buttercream with crushed peanuts around the outside.

To the Dressels, construction and creation of the cake was just as important as the taste. Everything needed to be local. The eggs all came in the shell and from a single nearby farmer. All the butter came from another single supplier and so did the high-butterfat cream—which Herman would accept only from Wisconsin Holsteins. The cream was pasteurized at the bakery, and then Herman developed a proprietary process to add even more butter into the cream.

The way the cake was made was innovative as well. The fudge layers had finely crushed carrot pulp in them because it helped keep them moist, and they were also made with oil instead of butter to help achieve that melt-in-your-mouth quality. The buttercream had vegetable shortening in it so it would be lighter than traditional buttercream, and they stabilized the whipped cream with agar-agar to make it firmer.

Herman's creation brought Chicagoans out in droves. By 1929, they needed two police officers at the bakery on Saturdays to handle the crowds. The Dressels were selling up to $3,000 worth of whipped cream cake in a single day, at either $0.60, $0.75 or $1.00 per cake. By the 1940s, ten thousand cakes a week were heading out the bakery doors. Dressel's had ten phone lines just to handle the incoming orders. The chocolate fudge whipped cream cake was outselling all the company's other cakes by 60 percent to 40 percent.

In order to meet demand, the Dressel brothers had to figure out a way to make the cakes in advance but have them still turn out great when it was time to eat. Prior to World War II, they began to experiment with freezing the cake layers. And from that experimentation emerged the Dressel's Frigi-Freez whipped cream cake. It came in three flavors: chocolate fudge, strawberry and banana. They were packaged in red and white boxes and sold in the freezer aisle in the grocery store.

The cakes became a ubiquitous part of every celebration around Chicagoland. Some people even kept a Dressel's cake in their freezer at all times. By the early 1960s—it was around 1963—William and Joseph had retired and sold the business to American Bakeries Inc. Herman stayed on for the transition. The new company wanted to expand distribution of the whipped cream cakes, hence the grocery store placement.

Herman played a major role in the future of the cakes. He worked in the production facility every day, brought home recipe samples for his family to try in the evenings, kept track of new baking ideas on a notepad in his pocket and helped develop new recipes.

"We were kind of his tasting panel of different things. It was fun," Herman's son Dan Dressel once said. "He was a well-known person in the industry and very sought after as far as his knowledge and innovation."

Herman worked at the bakery until he was eighty-two. Five years later, American Bakeries sold the Dressel's line to a French company, Pain Jacquet. It was a mistake. The company went deep into debt, going bankrupt in 1995 and ending production of the whipped cream cakes. Herman's family, though, never told him what happened. They didn't want him to know his company, his pride and joy, had such a depressing demise. Herman died in 1997, never learning about the bankruptcy.

Fans of Dressel's cakes knew, though, and were devastated to no longer have whipped cream cakes for celebrations. That is, until 2009. Wolf's Bakery in Evergreen Park worked together with the Dressel family to create as close a replica as possible to the old cake, and it's one of their bestsellers.

FROM DRESSEL'S RECIPE BOX

Chocolate Fudge Whipped Cream Cake (as developed by *Lost Recipes Found*)

Fudge Cake Ingredients

2 cups sugar
3 large eggs
1 ¼ cup vegetable oil
4 teaspoons vanilla
1 ⅓ cups boiling water
½ cup Hershey's Special Dark cocoa powder
1 ½ teaspoons baking soda
¾ teaspoon salt
1 ⅓ cups cake flour
1 cup all-purpose flour
1 cup toasted and ground mixed walnuts and pecans, for sides of finished cake

Whipped Cream Ingredients

1 cup water
½ teaspoon agar-agar
3 cups Kilgus Farmstead or other non-homogenized heavy cream (the closest approximation to what Dressel's used)
½ cup powdered sugar
1 teaspoon vanilla

Light Chocolate Buttercream Ingredients

2 cups room-temperature unsalted butter
½ cup vegetable shortening
4 cups powdered sugar
2 teaspoons vanilla
2½ tablespoons vegetable oil
4 tablespoons Dutch-process cocoa powder

Directions

Make the cake. Preheat oven to 350. Prepare two 9-inch baking pans by greasing them and lining them with parchment paper circles. In large mixing bowl, beat sugar and eggs 3 minutes until fluffy and creamy. Blend in oil and vanilla and beat 2 minutes more. Combine boiling water and cocoa powder and stir to dissolve. Mix in baking soda and salt. Pour into batter and incorporate. Add flours and mix until blended and smooth. Pour into prepared pans and tap pans on the counter to release bubbles. Bake at 350 for 35 to 40 minutes or until cake springs back when touched. Remove from oven; let rest in pans for five minutes. Turn onto racks. Let cakes cool completely.

While cake is baking, make the whipped cream. Place water in saucepan with agar-agar. Heat to boiling. Boil 4½ minutes. Let solution cool just until you can immerse your finger in it. It should still be quite warm and liquid; this takes about 3 to 3½ minutes. While you're waiting, combine cream with powdered sugar and vanilla and mix on low. Before cream reaches soft peak stage, add the warm agar-water solution and cream everything together. Whip until consistency firms up. The whipped cream will not be super firm, just firmer than typical whipped cream.

Make the light chocolate buttercream. Whip butter with vegetable shortening and powdered sugar at low speed for 8 to 10 minutes, until the mixture is fluffy. Add vanilla. Whip again to incorporate. Mix together oil and cocoa powder, and then whisk into buttercream until evenly distributed.

Assemble the cake. Trim the dome off the top of each fudge layer to ensure each layer is exactly level and of the same thickness. (If you are allergic to nuts, crumble this trim into crumbs and place on a parchment-lined baking sheet. Toast crumbs in the oven at 300 until crispy. Finely crush the crumbs and reserve.) Place first fudge cake layer on cake stand. Carefully pipe one inch of buttercream around the rim of the fudge layer, so you have a standing lip of buttercream on the cake. Fill this with a one-inch-tall layer of whipped cream. Add several more spoons of whipped cream onto the center. Place the second fudge cake layer over the whipped cream layer. Using an offset spatula, carefully seal the outside edge of the cake with buttercream, sealing the whipped cream in. Frost top of cake with buttercream. Frost sides of cake with buttercream. Apply nuts to sides of the cake, or, if allergic to nuts, use the toasted cake crumbs. Freeze the cake, which will ensure that the whipped cream layer and buttercream will firm up. Set cake out 30 to 45 minutes before serving to soften.

NAPLES BAKERY

3705 West 95th Street in Evergreen Park

On New Year's Eve 2016, Chicago lost a bakery that had been an enduring part of the community for nearly a century. That's the day Naples Bakery closed, ending generations of wedding cakes, turtle cookies, cannoli, napoleons and sfogiatellas satisfying the sweet tooth of locals. The closing came as a surprise to everyone, with a message posted on the bakery's Facebook page and on the door to make the announcement. And even though it was covered extensively in the media, to this day, people still expect the bakery to be there. Many of the bakers and customers interviewed for this book were unaware Naples had closed.

Naples was first opened by Italian immigrant Alphonso Lauro in 1918 on 67th and Wood Streets in the Englewood neighborhood. Later, he relocated the shop to a bigger building, at 69th Street and Paulina. There, Lauro launched a bread wholesale business, and the bakery supplied bread to nearly every restaurant on the south side. Lauro's son Joseph took over the business in the '50s. He started working there in his teens, driving delivery trucks. When he turned twenty (and after four years of service as a Navy baker during World War II), he took the helm.

The Icing on the Cake

Naples Bakery made the author's grandmother's wedding cake.

In 1963, Joseph moved the bakery to 95th Street in Evergreen Park. He had scouted locations for the new spot on every street south of 79th Street, going up and down the blocks. His ultimate choice was based on a simple feeling that he would enjoy that location—and he did. Joseph died in 2000, after he had passed the business to his daughter, Marijo Nowobielski, and her daughter, Jennifer Mavrogiannis. The recipes, all originating in Italy, were handed down along with the business.

Naples Bakery after the shop closed. *Courtesy of James Ward, stoneofzanzibar on Flickr.*

The family insisted there was no reason to be sad about the bakery's closing. Longtime customers shared story after story of their memories on social media and begged Naples not to close. But it wasn't to be.

"You know, if you put your life into it, of course it's sad," John Nowobielski, Marijo's husband, said at the time. "But also, you have to be happy. Because now we don't have to get up at 2:00 in the morning."

All told, Naples was open for ninety-seven years—quite an accomplishment for a small family business. The space was taken over by Barraco's Restaurant, longtime friends and colleagues of the team at Naples, whose building had been destroyed by a fire a few months before the bakery closed.

WAGNER'S BAKERY

2148 West Cermak Road in Heart of Chicago

When Jacob Wagner opened his bakery in 1918, the neighborhood was a mixture of Bohemian, German, Irish and Italian immigrants. He sold traditional European baked goods to local families—danishes, donuts, cookies and cakes. When he retired, he passed the business to his son Wayne. Then, around 2000, Wayne sold the business to Evequiel Flores. The neighborhood had transitioned to a Mexican community, and Flores had been a baker in Mexico before coming to Chicago with his son, Martin.

"Since I was five, I worked in bakeries in Mexico," said Martin, who now owns the bakery. "We came here in 1992 when I was fourteen years old. We worked in different bakeries around Chicago, then we bought Wagner's."

The Flores family changed up the offerings to appeal to both current and past customers. On the west side of the store, they stock traditional European baked goods, made from Wagner's old recipes. On the east side of the store, they have Mexican specialties. The current bestseller is Mexican concha bread, but Martin prefers to make custom cakes.

Cookies on display at Wagner's Bakery. *Author's collection.*

"It's so artistic," he said. "I like to see the people happy when they come for their cakes and they like it. I love to see their faces and smiles."

II

1920s to 1940s

These thirty years could be considered the heyday of Chicago bakeries. Many of the stalwarts still operating as family-owned bakeries opened during this time. Here we see the division of neighborhoods and ethnicities staying strong, but we also see the community begin to blend together and bakeries starting to sell more multicultural treats.

ANCONA BAKERY

3815 West Chicago Avenue in Humboldt Park

From the 1920s to the late 1950s, Humboldt Park residents flocked to John F. Buoniconti's Ancona Bakery for Italian treats like cannoli cake, cookies, Italian lemonade, cuccidati, bread and tiramisu. But then, on December 1, 1958, tragedy struck. A fire broke out at nearby Our Lady of the Angels grade school. It began in the basement of the school at about 2:15 p.m., quickly sweeping through the building, where 1,600 students were almost done with classes for the day. The lucky ones were near the back of a classroom, close to an exit or able to safely jump from a window. By the time the fire was out, 92 children and 3 nuns had lost their lives. More than 7,000 people attended the funerals. The cause of the blaze was never determined. It remains one of Chicago's worst fire tragedies and spurred updates to citywide fire codes.

The fire understandably cast a pall over Humboldt Park. One resident, Betti Wasek, shared her memories online:

> *The days and weeks to follow were filled with so much sadness. Our neighborhood would never ever be the same. We lived at 631 N. Avers which was 3 blocks south of the school. Everyone knew everyone and relatives lived either next door, across the street or even in the same building. On any summer evening you would see families sitting outside on their porches waiting for the peanut man with his cart or the man with horse and carriage giving the kids a ride around the block for ten cents a ride. You could walk down Chicago Ave. and get an Italian lemonade or cookies from Ancona's bakery….All of that was gone. The sights and sounds were replaced with an eerie quiet and family and friends eventually moved away. On our street alone, the Sarno and Mele families lost children. We were never allowed to talk about what had happened. We could not watch anything on TV that had to do with the fire. Radios were turned off. Newspapers were thrown away. It was almost as if people thought if we didn't talk about it anymore, it would go away. It did not and never will.*

Soon after the fire, Ancona Bakery left the neighborhood. The owners relocated to Melrose Park and then later to Northlake. Many Italian families were heading to those areas at the time, so it seemed a natural fit. And there, they were able to carry on for nearly sixty more years, eventually closing their doors in 2014.

DAVIDSON'S BAKERY

Multiple Locations

The next time you're watching *Blues Brothers*, pay attention during the Dixie Mall chase scene. As Jake and Elwood are barreling down Randolph, they pass a Davidson's Bakery. And when they get into the mall itself, a car crashes right into one before turning around and speeding away. The bakery's presence in the film is a testament to its popularity in Chicago.

Sam Davidson founded the company in the 1920s. By the time the company sold (along with all the recipes) to Heinemann's in 1982, there were fifteen stores around the city, most beneath or within eyesight of stops along

A Davidson's Bakery storefront. Note the sign on the door promoting "diet bread." *Public domain.*

the red line. They grew immensely popular for cheesecake, pies, donuts, honey cake, banana cake and flaky cheese strudel. Many of the storefront bakeries had terrazzo entryways emblazoned with a tiled "DB."

Davidson's had a mascot in the early years called Miss Cheese Cake, who was pictured in advertisements for the bakery, and the company advertised on cleverly designed matchbooks—every match depicted a standing chef, and the chef hats were the matchheads. The bakery was even featured in a book, *Sing a Song of Tuna Fish*, that collected author Esmé Raji Codell's fifth-grade memories. In the book, she says the cookies "were like tasting a candy cloud."

Davidson's desserts are regularly mentioned on message boards and social media pages as some of the most-missed Chicago foods. Those who miss the cheesecake might find a contender for it with the commonly found Sara Lee's cheesecake; Sam Davidson's brother-in-law was baker Charles Lubin, who opened a bakery in Chicago around 1950 and named his cheesecake line after his daughter, Sara Lee.

SARNO'S PASTRY SHOP

733 South Racine Avenue in Little Italy

In 1921, Frances and Umberto Sarno opened their bakery, Sarno's Pastry Shop, in Little Italy. They quickly gained popularity for danishes, cakes, Italian cookies and rum cake. Like most Italian bakeries at the time, Sarno's made massive wedding cakes complete with sugar lattice work and a dome on top that released doves when you cut into it. The best wedding cakes from Sarno's were modeled after churches in Europe.

In 1946, the Sarno family moved to Los Angeles. They sold their existing business to Andrew Salera, who then sold it to Anthony Allegretti, who moved the shop to Norridge in the 1960s and renamed it Allegretti's; his bakery is still open there. When Frances and Umberto arrived in LA, they quickly found a new building and reopened as a bakery with a coffeeshop next door, where employees sang opera for customers. It was run by Alberto Sarno, Frances and Umberto's son. In 1987, Alberto was followed home by would-be robbers who shot him to death. The café closed in 1991, and the bakery followed in 2000.

DINKEL'S BAKERY

3329 North Lincoln Avenue in Lakeview

Since 1922, Dinkel's Bakery has been supplying Chicago with all the stollen and German goodies customers could desire. The founder, Joseph Dinkel, and his wife, Antonie, arrived in Chicago around 1902 from Germany, where he had earned a master baker certification. Dinkel first got a job working for Schulze and Burch Biscuit Company. Around 1918, Dinkel's wife decided she didn't want to be in the United States anymore. So the two returned to Germany—and realized once they got there that it had changed and they didn't like it anymore. So, they returned to Chicago and opened the bakery. Joseph worked in the back baking, and Antonie handled the counter up front.

Antonie worked twelve to fourteen hours a day, bending down to get bread and pastries out of the cases. After a while, she got tired of bending down, so she created a new case called the Chicago Showcase. They were all

Above: Inside Dinkel's Bakery in the 1920s. *Dinkel's Bakery.*

Opposite: Joseph Dinkel, the founder of Dinkel's Bakery, posing with a tray of stollen. *Dinkel's Bakery.*

at counter height, so when a customer ordered something, she didn't have to bend over to get it—she just had to reach out in front of her. The bakery expanded in 1932, and those showcases were the most prominent feature in the upgrade.

Around this time, Joseph and Antonie's son, Norm Sr., came on board. Norm wasn't particularly interested in the business, but Joseph had been shot in a hold-up one Saturday night. So Norm Sr. dropped out of college and came to take over the bakery.

Back in those days, the bakery was open seven days a week, with the exception of Christmas.

"They'd be open from five in the morning to eleven every night, seven days a week, all the retail bakers, because people didn't have kitchens so they would shop at the bakery," said Norm Dinkel Jr., Joseph's grandson and the current owner of the bakery. "My mother would tell me that when she first got married, they were closed Christmas Day. Here's how they celebrated

Christmas: They'd work until 11:00 at night Christmas Eve. Then they'd shut down. So, these bakers worked like hell, got cleaned up, dressed in black tie, and got together at 12:30 a.m. for cocktails. Then they'd have a fabulous Christmas dinner presented at 2:00 a.m."

The German bakers in the city also loved to sing and dance, so they created a German Baker's Singing Society, which had branches all around the country. So they'd work all Friday night, and then Saturday, they'd go out and sing and dance all night long. "All the German bakers did that," Norm Jr. said.

Norm Dinkel Jr. on Disappearing Community Traditions

A lot of regular customers like to see the guy that owns the business. They know that it's still being managed by the family. But other traditions, I think that's what we're missing in this country. We don't have traditions anymore. I think the closest one we still get is Thanksgiving. That's one holiday everybody can celebrate. But I don't think it's celebrated too much anymore. More and more people go out because they don't want to cook. So, a lot of those traditions have fallen to the side. There's nothing I can do about it. I tried for years. I thought I could change the world. Now, I understand I can't change the world.

In the late 1950s, Dinkel's spearheaded another advancement in the bakery world. Norm Sr. invented the original unbaked frozen cheesecake. A grocery business eventually bought the rights to the cheesecake, and by 1962, it was rated the top frozen dessert by Consumer Reports.

Norm Jr. took over the bakery from his father in the early 1970s. He was a practicing lawyer at the time, and his dad wanted to retire. If he didn't pass it on, he was just going to sell the bakery. Norm Jr.'s attorney friends convinced him owning his own business was preferable to practicing law, so he moved into the bakery business.

At one time, the current bakery building was a paint shop—and in that store, Dutch Boy paints were first invented. It was torn down in 1886, and the current building replaced it in 1888. But remnants of the paint shop stayed.

"We had a basement downstairs," said Norm Jr. "There was an old sewer pit which was covered up and not in use. And we had one of the government agencies come out. This is before I knew about the paint store. They're going through, they're opening stuff up that hadn't been opened for well over one hundred years, taking samples. So, they came up with some terrible toxic stuff in this one pit. And the guy said, 'We're ready to shut you down. We're going to arrest you and throw you in jail. There are all kinds of chemicals in this thing.' I told him there were no chemicals like that in my whole business. Had I known, I could have told him that sewer pit is from the paint shop, and they probably dumped a lot of stuff down there."

Ultimately, the inspectors didn't find any trace of chemicals in the rest of the building. They let Norm Jr. off the hook. Which is good, because business was booming. On a typical day, Dinkel's sold about two thousand coffeecakes and eight hundred dozen sweet rolls. Around Easter time, it sold up to sixteen thousand lamb cakes. Some other popular items were danishes

Lincoln Avenue before Dinkel's opened, pictured around 1885. The bakery currently sits where the paint store is in the picture. *Dinkel's Bakery.*

and Irish soda bread (both still made today with the same recipe), dark bread, custard pies, pecan pies and stollen, which is still made today and was so popular it was featured in a book.

Today, the bakery includes a café that makes sandwiches. It was once a T-shirt store that renters operated, but the tenants weren't paying rent. One day, a dump truck lost control and plowed right into the store. Norm Jr. evicted the tenant and remodeled the shop into the café.

Moving back from the café into the kitchen, you can see the wall style changing when you pass into the original bakery—with the original flooring—from 1922. That's where the cakes are made today. You can follow the history of the building and its every expansion based on the floors and the walls. In the dishwashing area, the floors are still original and get so slick when they're wet that the bakers used to play hockey on them. On the second floor, there's a packaging area, a party space for kids' events and the production area for sweet rolls, coffeecakes, croissants and anything with puff pastry. According to Norm Jr., the bakery spends $10,000 a month—in the slow season—just on butter for these treats. Also

The Dinkel's Bakery storefront as it looks today, before the awning was added. *Dinkel's Bakery.*

upstairs is the apartment Norm Jr. grew up in, complete with the original kitchen, pink-tiled bathroom and stained glass windows. Another floor up, there once was a second apartment. That's where temporary employees stayed when Dinkel's started having a booth at Christkindlmarkt.

"I had to bring people in from the mountains because those were the only people I could find that would work the booth," Norm Jr. said.

Aside from the café, Dinkel's now does a brisk business selling donuts, brownies, cookies, cakes and more. Luke Karl, Norm Jr.'s son-in-law, is next in line to take over the bakery.

ALLIANCE BAKERY

1736 West Division Street in Wicker Park

In 2017, Alliance Bakery had a pretty special order: it got to make the cake for Chance the Rapper's birthday. The Chicago-born rapper's cake featured another Chicago staple in addition to being made by Alliance; it was a Harold's Chicken–themed cake. The dessert was two tiers—the bottom with the Harold's logo and the top with a box of faux fries and a cascade of surprisingly realistic chicken wings slathered in hot sauce.

This mind-bending birthday cake wasn't the first specialty order handled by Alliance, though. The bakery has been building cakes and creating sweet bites on Division Avenue since 1923. It was originally a Polish bakery to match the makeup of the neighborhood at the time, selling fresh bread and Polish dessert mainstays. The original name of the bakery is up for debate; it was either always Alliance, or it was first named after the Sompolski family that owned it and then updated to Alliance when they sold it around the 1940s. A variety of bakers have owned the spot (including Heidi Hedeker of Gladstone Park Bakery fame), but now Peter Rios, a Paris-trained pastry chef, is at the helm.

"There are a lot of old bakeries in Europe that have been passed on through generations," Rios said. "And in Chicago, Alliance Bakery built a great foothold. Occasionally people have brought in their own photos to show and say, hey, I grew up here when I was kid in the '40s or '50s, and here's a picture of me. The community went through a series of ups and downs throughout the hundred years the bakery has been here, through

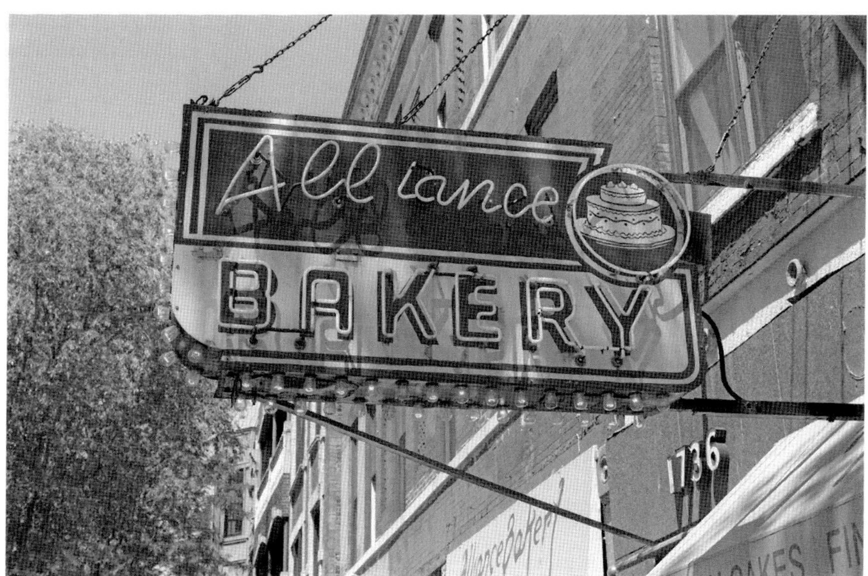

The Alliance Bakery sign. *Steven Miller.*

Chef Peter Rios on the Enduring Power of Bread

[Bakeries are] essential to basic human needs. They've been able to endure wars, pandemics, and other types of social unrest, because people will always want their bread or their pastries. All the bakeries in Chicago, and even around the world, didn't specialize in just sweets or desserts. They specialized in breads with sweets, and bread, being a basic need for humanity, is never going to go away. It's not a fickle item. Bread supersedes anything retail or modern. It goes way back through civilization. There's always been a need for the baker.

some bad times and rough times, and now it's gotten a revitalization with the more urbanized and gentrified crowd."

And with the change in audience, the products have changed as well. Gone are the traditional pączki and kolaches—Rios says the demand for those waned to almost nothing over the years. In their place, Alliance's shelves are stocked with French and American staples like almond croissants, apple fritters, macarons, butter cookies, kouign-amann and red velvet cupcakes. In 2011, Rios introduced a series of anti–Valentine's Day cookies, toting slogans like "stop calling me" and "it's not me, it's you." His team is always pushing to new pastry heights in a continuing effort to thrive in an ever-changing bakery world.

REUTER'S BAKERY

7177 West Grand Avenue in Galewood

From a newly married couple missing their honeymoon to one of the most historic bakeries in Chicago, the story of Reuter's Bakery is one of passion, tradition and hard work. It was first opened in 1927 by Leo Reuter and his wife, Hanna, with money that was set aside for their honeymoon and first home together. It was a risky venture; Leo had been in the country less than a decade at that point, and when he arrived, he had just one suitcase with him. But the risk paid off. The couple dove into the business headfirst, becoming popular not just for their baked goods, but also for their community involvement. Reuter's quickly became the largest retail bakery in Chicago, with seventy-two employees on the payroll.

After forty years, the Reuters retired. Leo sold the business to a longtime customer, Richard Eberle, in 1967. Luckily, Eberle saw the value of keeping the business in the family. In 2000, he passed the business on to his son, Richard Jr., who now runs the shop with his wife, Erin.

The bakery remains a neighborhood institution, bringing in generations of the same families to buy scratch-made coffeecake, bread, tortes, cookies, donuts and more. Employees know all the regulars and can bag their orders almost instinctively, and many of the products are made using same recipes Leo and Hanna did when started their lives together there.

"My notion is that it's about consistency," Eberle Jr. said. "We make the product over and over again, the same way. People identify with it, and they come back because they know it's a good product. Now, I think it caters to everybody. We have items that are Italian, we do pączki, we do zeppoles for St. Joseph's Day. We're here for everybody."

SWEDISH BAKERY

5348 North Clark Street in Andersonville

Starting in 1928, Andersonville's Swedish Bakery was an icon in the neighborhood and a destination for tourists from around the country. There was always a line of people patiently waiting for the best Swedish sweets in Chicago: weinerbrod custard pastries, forty varieties of traditional cookies, cardamom braids, lemon rolls, cherry strudel, butter cookies, limpa bread, marzipan and the local favorite, a princess cake. The cake was three layers, sponge cake separated first by raspberry filling and then again by pastry cream and stiffly whipped cream. Then the entire thing was covered in a layer of green marzipan.

The bakery went through five owners during its time in Andersonville. The Johnson family first opened it in 1928, and then they sold it to Ernest Carlson in 1940. In 1964, it changed hands again, to Gosta Bjuhr. He hired the next owner, Marlies Stanton, who worked there for eight years and eventually bought the bakery from Bjuhr in 1979. After she passed, her daughter Kathy took over. After an expansion in 1992, it became one of the largest family-owned bakeries in Chicago, with fifty-five employees.

Under Stanton's ownership, the bakery helped celebrate milestones in Chicago. They helped host journalist Studs Terkel's one hundredth birthday party a few years after his death, and they celebrated the Michigan Avenue Bridge's ninety-fourth anniversary with a cake in the bridge's Gear Room.

The Swedish Bakery storefront in Andersonville. *Juhan Sonin.*

Swedish Bakery former owner Gosta Bjuhr making lussikat, a Santa Lucia Day pastry. *Library of Congress.*

Swedish Bakery former owner Gosta Bjuhr holding a cake that says "Volkommen Harry." *Library of Congress.*

They gave back to the community as well; surplus from daily sales was sent to the St. Gregory Church monastery.

By the time Swedish Bakery closed its doors in 2017, it had been in operation for eighty-eight years and was the only Swedish bakery left in Chicago. No younger Stantons were around to take over the business, which was suffering in the modern era. They closed on Pączki Day, drawing a 120-person-deep line. All is not lost, though—the Bryn Mawr Breakfast Club's baker makes several of the recipes from his thirty-six years at the Swedish Bakery, Lost Larson re-creates the princess cake and Bennison's Bakery sells Swedish Bakery favorite the Andersonville Coffeecake.

GLADSTONE PARK BAKERY

5744 North Milwaukee Avenue in Jefferson Park

When Dean Hedeker (whose legal name was Daniel) arrived in Chicago from Germany in 1952, he was nineteen, broke and spoke no English. One day he walked into a bakery looking for a job, and before he knew it, he was in the back frying up donuts.

That bakery was Gladstone Park. It was opened in 1929 by a German couple, who then passed it on to baker Ronald Rapp in 1952, the same year Hedeker came on board. At the time, the only employees were Rapp, his mother and Hedeker. As time went on, Rapp expanded the business and hired more employees, and Hedeker learned English, married a woman named Lina and started his family.

Rapp was an exemplary boss, mentoring not just his staff but their children as well.

"One day a year, he would have all the kids of the bakers come and work on-site," Dean and Lina's daughter Heidi, onetime owner of Alliance Bakery, said. "They put me on a milk crate and had me dipping spritz cookies. I was about four years old, so I would break a lot of them. So Ron, I'll never forget, he came over and asked, 'What's going on over there?' I had a great idea that the broken cookies should be on sale. I told Ron, 'Well, I think you should sell them at half price.' I will never forget the look on his face, which was both like he was going to absolutely kill me and also that it was a great idea. He laughed it off. But I got a feeling, even at that age, that this was fun and games but that it also sort of wasn't."

The same day every year that Rapp had the kids working in the bakery, he also sent them out with trays of cookies to hand out to customers. At the end of the day, he gave them each a dollar bill with a handwritten thank-you note tucked into an envelope.

Over the years, Dean rose in the ranks from donut fryer to foreman of the entire bakery. Rapp was so appreciative that he sent Dean and Lina on a trip to Europe. He sent a letter, on glimmering gold Gladstone Park Bakery letterhead, to the rest of the employees after they'd left for the trip:

> *20 years ago, a young man on a winter day in February came in for a job, and since that time has come to be known as our foreman at Gladstone Park Bakery.*
>
> *In appreciation for the excellent job he has done over the years, and as a special thank you to his wife, Dean Hedeker and Lina are now en route to Vienna, Austria where Dean will represent Gladstone at the International Bakery Exposition. In addition to this trip, there will be stopovers in London and Rome.*
>
> *The special thanks given to Lina is for the flexibility in their home life and is also given to all of the wives of our bakers who help make it easier for them to be available at Gladstone Park Bakery each day.*
>
> *Also, I am sorry if this letter is a surprise to you but all of you know of the situations that can arise at the bakery—illness, machinery breakdowns, etc.—which may have kept Dean here.*
>
> *Sincerely, Ron*
>
> *P.S. Dean will return the beginning of October.*

Rapp got cancer when he was in his late forties. He went to Dean and offered the business up for sale. By that time, the bakery had fifty employees and was doing well over $1 million in sales every year. In 1973, Rapp died and Dean took over. Dean, Lina and their children moved into the apartment above the bakery.

"My dad had the rags-to-riches situation," Heidi said. "He came over here with literally just a suitcase and couldn't speak English and then owned this multimillion-dollar business. He really enjoyed his life."

Within three years, the specialty cake business was booming, in addition to the already brisk sales of babka, coffeecakes and rolls. On an average weekend day, more than four hundred specialty cakes—in all shapes and sizes—were heading out the bakery's doors. Dean noted that they could make anything—all someone had to do was bring in a picture. The cakes

Gladstone Park

GLADSTONE PARK BAKERY
5744 Milwaukee Avenue ◆ Chicago, Illinois 60646
Phone SPring 4-4210 - 4-4211

Foreman Trip to Europe

20 years ago, a young man on a winter day in February came in for a job, and since that time has come to be known as our foreman at Gladstone Park Bakery.

In appreciation for the excellent job he has done over the years, and as a special thank you to his wife, Dean Hedeker and Lina are now in route to Vienna, Austria where Dean will represent Gladstone at the International Bakery Exposition. In addition to this trip, there will be stopovers in London and Rome.

The special thanks given to Lina is for the flexibility in their home life and is also given to all of the wives of our bakers who help make it easier for them to be available at Gladstone Park Bakery each day.

Also, I am sorry if this letter is a surprise to you but all of you know of the situations that can arise at the bakery - illness, machinery breakdowns, etc. - which may have kept Dean here.

Sincerely,

Ron

P.S. Dean will return the beginning of October.

(Dean plane leaves monday night 730)

Personalized Order Service

Decorated Cakes while-u-wait — Four Bread Bakings Daily

Visit our Wedding Cake Room — Continuous Daylight Baking

A letter from Ron Rapp to Gladstone Park Bakery staff about Dean Hedeker's trip to Europe. *Heidi Hedeker.*

were shaped like everything you could imagine: animals, sports equipment, cars, clowns, instruments and more.

In the early 2000s, Jefferson Park was beginning to change, and Dean didn't think he could keep up with it. So he kept the property but sold the bakery itself to a group of people who had never been bakers.

"That didn't mean it couldn't work, but it didn't work," Heidi said. "That was really sad. It was a long, drawn-out ten or fifteen years of mismanagement by the new owners. Word got around within a year that they weren't making things by hand on premises anymore. They lost all their business."

They'd also been paying rent sporadically, stringing along Lina, who was in her eighties, without giving her the ability to evict them. The city eventually shut down the bakery in 2008, finding more than six hundred mice droppings in the mixing, baking and storage areas. Mice had even chewed through bags of flour. The closure allowed Lina to finally evict the new owners, and she regained the business license from them as well.

The bakery stayed closed for about three years. After Lina died, Heidi and her brothers sold the property. It recently reopened as an Italian bakery, helmed by a brother and sister baking duo.

HEINEMANN'S BAKERIES

Multiple Locations

In 1929, the Heinemann family opened a small bakery on the north side. It was known then for producing quality products with no preservatives; they baked everything they sold the day of the sale, so nothing sat out to get stale. Heinemann's was so popular that by 1935, it had a chain of three stores. At that point, the Heinemann family sold the small chain to locals Anton Dorner and Charles Meyering. (The Heinemanns went on to open bakeries and restaurants of the same name in Milwaukee, but the two companies were no longer related.) By 1942, when Meyering died, he and Dorner had expanded the company to include nine more stores.

Dorner took over the whole business that year, bringing on his two sons, Ernest and Herbert. In 1959, the Dorners invented the in-store bakery concept. They launched a self-service bakery inside a Dominick's grocery store, under the Heinemann's Bakeries name. Five years later, they acquired another bakery, Hillman Bakery, and stepped up the grocery store business, eventually having retail bakeries in 150 stores around the country. Demand was so high that they had to expand into a new plant at 1902 West Bryn Mawr Avenue.

The Dorners passed the company to their family and have since passed away. But Heinemann's Bakeries products live on. A range of items, including cakes, coffeecakes, cookies and hot cross buns, are available at Jewel grocery stores.

HAAS BAKERY

3056 North Milwaukee Avenue in Avondale

Haas Bakery was a true family business. Adolph and Pauline Haas opened it in the 1930s after immigrating from Austria and operating a previous bakery in the city. It was a good decision; the couple ran the bakery until the 1950s, when they transferred ownership to their son, Edward Haas, and his wife, Ruth. Edward and Ruth continued to run it until the 1970s. Edward was born in Adolph and Pauline's first bakery on Armitage, which is now Dee's restaurant. He died in 2013.

The family lived in the upstairs of the Milwaukee Avenue spot, and everyone worked at the bakery—including Adolph and Pauline's son Adolph; his wife, Helen; and their daughter Nancy. The younger Adolph and Pauline opened their own bakery in Niles in the 1960s. It burned down on New Year's Eve, 1964. He rebuilt by May 1965 and eventually opened another location in Des Plaines in the 1970s.

In September 2011, fire struck again, burning down the original building Haas Bakery was in. The business was long since closed and replaced by a Polish bakery, but family and community members still mourned the loss.

HOPFNER'S BAKERY

4754 North Lincoln Avenue in Lincoln Square

In the 1930s, Anthony G. Hopfner opened a German bakery in the heart of Lincoln Square. A few years after Hopfner's opened, Anthony's soon-to-be wife, Audrey, began working there as a supervisor. Audrey, who moved to Chicago from suburban Waukegan, became a fixture in the store.

The bakery was known for German specialties like kuchen, bread and brownies—and for Audrey's unfailing kindness and good nature. She always lent a helping hand as needed, like when there was a massive snowstorm in 1967. The family lived in nearby Sauganash at the time. All the roads and businesses were closed due to the storm, but the local grocery store needed to stay open. Audrey was there to lend a hand, filling in as a cashier and sending her sons out to deliver groceries by sled.

April Fool's Day was a hit at Hopfner's because Audrey and other longtime employees liked to prank the bakers. Friend and co-worker Rita Unger, who worked at the bakery for thirty years, recalled the two of them tying the bakers' shoelaces together when they weren't paying attention and then watching them fall over.

Hopfner's closed in 1973, when Anthony and Audrey retired to Florida.

LEVINSON'S BAKERY

2856 West Devon Avenue in West Rogers Park

Back in the 1950s and 1960s, Levinson's Bakery was one of several kosher Jewish bakeries on Devon Avenue. It was also one of the oldest. The bakery has been operating for more than eighty years and is still in the same location. It was first opened by Molly and Phillip Levinson. One of the past owners, Ben Neiman, was a Holocaust survivor from Novobarovo, Ukraine.

The sign at Levinson's Bakery. *Thomas Hawk.*

During its generations of operation, Levinson's has become famous for Jewish staples like challah, mandelbrot, babka and poppy seed rolls. The bakery is also popular for items like braided coffeecakes, honey cakes, sweet egg dough rolls, pistachio cannoli, pumpernickel bread and strudels.

NELSON'S BAKERY

2245 West Devon Avenue in West Rogers Park

Though the space is now an art gallery, Nelson's Bakery, known for its cakes and rolls, opened during the Swedish bakery boom on the north side around the 1930s. There were at least six in the area in those early days. They were competitive, sure, but community came first. Together, they formed a Swedish Bakers Association that not only networked and threw picnics for the bakers and their families but also worked out operating schedules. The bakeries wanted to ensure that when each owner's family took a vacation in the summer, none of the shops would be closed at the same time.

WEBER'S BAKERY

7055 West Archer Avenue in Garfield Ridge

With Mike Weber at the helm, Weber's Bakery in Garfield Ridge is on its third generation of family ownership. Erich H. Weber came to Chicago from Germany in 1924, taking odd jobs at bakeries in the city. In 1930, he opened his own shop at 45th and Kedzie, on the southwest side.

In the early days, Weber's gained its footing in the community thanks to scratch-made desserts and bread, like rye bread, kolache, pumpkin pie, pound cake, carrot cake and chocolate donuts. Weber also helped start a secret society of bakers in Chicago called the Bakers Dozen, a group that still operates today. The thirteen members are noncompetitive bakers from Chicagoland who meet regularly to share ideas, recipes, concerns and problems in their bakeries.

By 1937, Weber realized he needed a larger building, so he moved the bakery to 63rd Street and St. Louis Avenue. In 1957, his son, Erich R. Weber, took over the bakery, building a second shop at the bakery's current location in 1979. The 63rd Street bakery has since been torn down.

About the time the younger Erich took over, the atomic cake (a layered cake stuffed with bananas, Bavarian cream, banana custard, strawberries and strawberry cream) was gaining steam on the southwest side—and only the southwest side.

Inside Weber's Bakery in the 1930s. *Weber's Bakery.*

Mike Weber's grandmother inside the 63rd Street bakery in the 1930s. They used to sell eggs and milk in addition to baked goods. *Weber's Bakery.*

Erich H. Weber at the oven in Weber's Bakery. *Weber's Bakery.*

> The Icing on the Cake
>
> The author has been eating Weber's Bakery delights since she was a child, and her extended family adores the bakery.

"[The atomic cake] seems to be a southwest side thing," Mike (the younger Erich's son) said. "There was a bakery on the north side, Gladstone Park Bakery, that was almost the north side version of us. They were like a mirror. [The owner,] Dean Hedeker, would tell my dad, 'Well I can't sell that atomic cake up here.' But he could make it just as good as us."

Weber's wanted to come up with a recipe to differentiate it from the pack of other bakeries, so it created the banana split torte.

"A lot of places do a banana, chocolate, and yellow dough on top, and that's the atomic," Mike said. "Ours is the banana split torte because the banana cake is split, so the top and bottom is banana. And we always use fresh fruit. I've seen guys try to sell it without using fresh strawberries. They use frozen strawberries or they use custard that isn't from scratch, and they don't sell as well."

Ever since the two Erichs created the cake, it's been the go-to bestselling cake at the bakery.

Mike grew up in the bakery, and one of things he's noticed over the years is that customers have no qualms about sharing their opinions when something changes. In the 1970s, for example, the sugar Weber's used in the icing for its chocolate donuts got incredibly expensive. So Erich R. changed the recipe a little, tweaking it to use a different sugar. Customers caught on immediately, and within a week, they were pressuring the bakery to go back to the old sugar—which it did, despite the high cost.

"They know there's a Weber walking past them in the store and they don't have a problem saying, 'Hey, Weber, get over here. What's with this, or why did you stop making that,'" Mike said. "You're not going to do that at Jewel. You're not going to ask the guy behind the Jewel counter why they stopped making something or why something isn't what it used to be. I think that's why people consider us their bakery, and that's what we want it to be."

The donut snafu is far from Mike's favorite memory, though. He shared a story of one Thanksgiving around 1966, when there was an ice storm. People couldn't pick up their pies, so his dad was stuck with a ton of Thanksgiving pies. To get rid of the excess, he brought Mike and some of his brothers into the shop and let them have a pie fight. Mike maintains that none of them won the fight—but their dad definitely lost, because he had to clean everything up.

Weber's Bakery used to make A-frame gingerbread houses. No other bakery made a similar one. *Weber's Bakery.*

In 1997, the younger Erich retired, and Mike took over. Now, Mike works there with his daughter, Becky, who will be the fourth generation of ownership when he retires.

"We've changed dramatically over the years," Mike said. "If somebody came in then and came in now, they wouldn't even recognize it. The whole retail bakery business has changed in Chicago in the last ninety-one-plus years. Many things, though, haven't changed, like tradition and being a scratch bakery, where we still make all our products from scratch."

The bakery's popularity continues to grow. Weber's was named the best bakery in Illinois by *Business Insider*, something Mike is proud of. It has made

Mike Weber in the bakery. *Weber's Bakery.*

Erich R. Weber with a City of Chicago birthday cake. *Weber's Bakery.*

Mike Weber on the Bakers Dozen

My grandfather was one of the founding members in the 1940s. He and a bunch of bakers who were not competitors established it. It was a monthly meeting at a different guy's shop. He would request three items, so let's say his rye bread wasn't coming out. He would say, I want you to bring your rye bread and your formula [recipe]. Then they'd stand around the table, they'd talk about it, they'd taste it, and then he would get ideas to make his better. It's changed a lot over the years but it's been probably the most valuable tool we've had.

The thing about that group is restaurants are a different animal from bakeries and bakeries are different than other retail businesses because it's food. Having a group of people that understands your life, your trials, your tribulations is just so invaluable. And even when you go to a meeting, maybe you don't get any product ideas because you say well, ours is better than any of those. But somebody might say one sentence that causes you to think about how you're doing something, maybe a process you're doing that could be more efficient, or a piece of equipment that someone got that is helping them. So it's been really, really important.

It was so far ahead of its time when I think about it, even now. And what's great now is even though sometimes we may have to skip a meeting, if there's a snowstorm or this or that, the meetings are unimportant—because with text messaging and emails, there's a meeting every day. If I'm having a problem with something, I can text twelve, fourteen people immediately and get their feedback. And then we need the group for ingredients. I know a lot of our distributors don't like it because sometimes someone will say, "Hey, what are you paying for eggs?" And then the numbers come back and you realize, wait a minute, I'm getting charged too much by my supplier. So they may not like it, but it keeps their pencil sharpened.

cakes for celebrities and almost always has a line out the door. Pączki sales have jumped from twenty pans on Pączki Day in 1981 to tens of thousands of pączki now. The bakery has become known as a Chicago tradition.

"We take it personally," Mike said. "I think that's one of the things about a family business, we do take it personally. My wife always says, 'You realize we're at people's Easter table, we're at their Christmas breakfast, their Christmas dinners.' It's special, you know?"

Mike Weber's daughter, Becky, who plans to take over the bakery when he retires. *Weber's Bakery.*

REYNEN'S BAKERY

3056 North Southport Avenue in Lakeview

Walking into Reynen's Bakery in the 1990s was like stepping back in time. The bakery was opened by Albert and Helene Reynen in 1931. They got married in June and opened the shop in October, right in the middle of the Great Depression. And until the day the bakery closed in 1996, time inside was frozen in the past. Everything was made from scratch, without massive equipment or machines. Milk, butter and juice occupied an operational cooler from the 1920s with "Whipped Cream Cakes" emblazoned on the top. Orders for cookies were weighed out on a cast-iron balance, piled onto one side and measured with a lead weight on the other. Even the cash register was a throwback to earlier times. It was made during the Depression and could count up only to $3.99—because bakery orders never cost more than that at the time. Everything sold at Reynen's was wrapped in baker's paper and string, and it was most likely bought from Helene, who took over operations once Albert died in 1989. He was eighty-four when he died and still working and keeping a baker's hours, working throughout the night to make sure bread and other treats would be ready by morning. Helene was a piece of the old days as well, always clad in beige tennis shoes, a dress and smock and pearls. She didn't believe in pants on women at work, she didn't wear makeup, and she didn't own a washer and dryer, instead preferring to use a washtub and clothesline.

"You can just tell she's been in this room for 150 years, and that's nice," customer John Oster said in 1994, on one of his regular Saturday morning visits. He'd been coming in for fifteen years to buy apricot kolackys and upside-down chocolate cupcakes. "And this place, you can just tell it's been here forever, and I hope it stays forever. It's like a constant, and there are so few constants."

The Reynens' children all grew up in the bakery, learning to ride bikes and read by the glow of the big brick oven in the back. Two of the sons, Willy and Albert Jr., helped out and ran the bakery with their parents until their sixties. Some of the bestsellers included nut bars, peach kuchen, raspberry claws and oatmeal cookies. The potato rolls were particularly popular, especially on Sundays after church—the Reynens sold about sixty-five dozen of those some mornings. Lines would stretch around the bakery, out the door and down the street.

On the holidays, four generations piled into the bakery to help bake, decorate, package and sell products. All the traditional German favorites would make an appearance on the shelves—Bavarian spice cookies, stollen, basala lebkuchen. The littlest kids got to sprinkle toppings like chopped cherries onto the treats. It was a point of pride for the Reynen family to have everyone there at once. The women (Helene, and Willy and Albert Jr.'s wives) even nicknamed themselves "the store girls."

The bakery closed up shop after Helene died in 1996. But the Reynen's tradition is carried on by Albert and Helene's granddaughter Tricia, who runs a bakery in the suburbs without a storefront that sells at farmers markets and takes special orders. She uses some of the same recipes from Reynen's in her business, Tricia's Bake Shop.

TUZIK'S 95TH STREET BAKERY

4955 West 95th Street in Oak Lawn

The story of Tuzik's 95th Street Bakery is one that unfortunately ends in tragedy. The bakery was first opened in 1931 by Ted Tuzik's grandparents, immigrants from Poland. Their original shop was in the city proper, in Gage Park on the southwest side, at 53rd and Kedzie. It stayed in that location until 1981 when Ted, the third-generation owner, moved it to Oak Lawn with his business partner and brother-in-law Bill Love. Over the years, the bakery gained local fame for treats like donuts, pączki, lamb cakes, rye bread, cookies, sweet rolls and Irish soda bread.

On Halloween 2019, Ted unexpectedly died. He had just turned sixty-eight earlier that month. Staff made the decision to close the bakery permanently after his passing. Ted was irreplaceable to them—and to many members of the community—and no one wanted to continue on in the business without him.

BAYS ENGLISH MUFFIN CORPORATION

1026 West Jackson Boulevard in Greektown

In 1933, a breakfast tradition began in Chicago. George W. Bay opened a small bakery in the South Loop, selling ladyfingers, crumpets, bread and English muffins from a secret family recipe. The recipe belonged to Bay's grandmother, who brought it to the United States in the 1800s when she emigrated from England.

Business quickly whittled down to just the English muffins, as demand for those far outweighed demand for the other products. Bay sold them in paper bags and hand-delivered them around the city to grocery stores and private clubs. Customers loved the light and airy texture resulting from the heirloom recipe and its then-secret ingredient: potato flour. It was as authentic as Bay could get; in England at the turn of the century, bakers used mashed potatoes and bread to make their muffins. In 1938, the company graduated from the bags and began selling the English muffins in a box with a cellophane window. Bays was one of the first companies to ever do that.

Business continued to grow through the 1950s, even as interest in English muffins waned in their homeland, England. There's a rumor that the queen herself had to find a private supplier because muffin men, local street vendors selling the muffins, were no longer around. But that rapidly disappearing English charm is part of what kept Bays popular. People liked the Gothic red-and-white logo, they liked the authentic recipe, they liked thinking their English muffins actually came from England. And they liked the other things that set Bays apart from other companies—the muffins were (and still are)

Tom Robaczewski, VP of Sales at Bays Bakery Incorporated, on All the Uses of Bays English Muffins, as Told to *Business in Focus*

Everyone's familiar with the English muffin as an accompaniment of breakfast or for a breakfast sandwich, but there are a lot of other usages for English muffins. It's a great snack item with butter, bananas or cream cheese on it. And it works great for making sandwiches with lunchmeat, peanut butter and jelly or virtually anything. Pizzas are also a popular use for English muffins; I remember when growing up, our family made little mini pizzas on Friday nights with Bays English Muffins. And one of the best usages that I've recently come across was to use them with burgers. There's just something about a burger—that when you grill it, the juices from the burger get absorbed into the English muffin, and it makes the perfect combination.

sold in the refrigerated case by the eggs and milk rather than the bread aisle, and they're all completely sliced rather than fork-split.

"This provides a crisp edge around it, once toasted, and allows butter to melt down into the muffin, making some terrific sandwiches," Tom Robaczewski, the current vice president of sales, said in 2018.

In 1968, George's son, James Sr., took over operations at the bakery. He made two big advancements. First, he moved the bakery to a new location in an old needle factory by the Sears Tower. Second, he partnered with McDonald's. In 1972, McDonald's chairman Ray Kroc came to James Sr. with a proposal. He was local and had grown up eating Bays English muffins. How about a new breakfast sandwich at McDonald's, he suggested, using a Bays English muffin as the bread? James Sr. agreed, and the Egg McMuffin was born. Demand for Bays went wild after that. It got so busy that James Sr.'s sons, James Jr. and George, decided to leave the independent careers they were carving out to come work at the bakery. James Sr. died in 1997; his sons were already fully in charge of the business by that point. McDonald's used Bays to make the sandwiches until 1984.

Business continued to boom regardless, with the factory now pumping out up to 400,000 English muffins daily and selling in thirty-six states and a handful of countries. For a time, they had a second bakery facility in Detroit, but that has since closed.

In 2017, the Bay family sold the business to Bimbo Bakeries USA, which then renamed the company to Bays Bakery Incorporated. Almost immediately, customers began to question the quality of the English muffins under the new ownership. They were concerned the recipe

A bag of Bays English Muffins before they introduced resealable packaging. *Creative Commons.*

had changed; the consistency was supposedly not as soft, with fewer air bubbles. It reached the point that Bimbo had to issue a statement in early 2021 noting that the recipe is still the same and the only difference now is the packaging.

That packaging, though, was a win for customers. For years, they'd complained the bags weren't resealable, leading to wasted muffins. Bimbo took that to heart and in 2020 introduced resealable packaging.

BENNISON'S BAKERY

1000 Davis Street in Evanston

Bennison's Bakery may not be in Chicago, but its location in Evanston makes it a longtime favorite for many people on the north side of the city. The bakery began as an in-store supermarket bakery chain for Red Owl, a grocery store business in Minneapolis, in 1934. Red Owl wanted to expand to thirteen stores around Chicago. John Bennison, whom everyone called Larry, contracted with them to operate the bakeries. Bennison built a bakery in Wheeling to handle the incoming store orders and set up several of his employees with their own in-store bakeries.

Red Owl opened two or three stores in the area, but they weren't successful. The grocery chain abandoned the project, leaving Bennison out in the cold. He had three bakeries at that time with space for ten more and took a severe financial beating when the grocery chain backed out. He ended up in a lot

Guy Downer, then owner of Bennison's Bakery, giving a decorating demonstration at a local school. *Bennison's Bakery.*

of debt. Because of his contract with Red Owl, he couldn't make baked goods for anyone but Hackney's Restaurants and the Red Owl stores, so he was unable to make enough money to cover his costs. A college friend eventually had to help bail Bennison out.

After the Red Owl debacle settled, Bennison owned three bakeries and baked in two. The two he baked in were both in Evanston, one on Central Street and one on Davis Street, where the current location of the bakery remains. By now it was 1962, and at the time, the American Institute of Baking was in Chicago. Bennison was taking meetings down at the Institute when he met Guy Downer, a sales representative for Standard Brands, which sold Fleischmann's Yeast to bakeries in and around Chicago. Bennison suggested to Downer that he leave the sales world and come run some of the bakery. Just as Downer decided to accept the offer, Bennison abruptly died. The bakeries floated for about a year while his family tried to sell the business. They never found anyone, though, and eventually called Downer and sold the entire operation to him. Downer took over in the 1960s, with his son Jory joining him at the bakeries after high school. Eventually, the Bennison's Bakery business blossomed to eight stores around Chicagoland.

Above: Guy Downer (*left*) and Jory Downer standing together in the Bennison's Bakery production area. *Bennison's Bakery.*

Left: This image of Guy Downer measuring flour into a scale was used for the scale company's marketing materials. *Bennison's Bakery.*

Jory Downer on the Bakers Dozen

It's like the Skull and Bones of the bakery world. There are thirteen members, and we meet the first Wednesday of every month. Whoever hosts the meeting typically picks three items to talk about. They're items that you're having trouble with, things you're not pleased with that you're making. Then we go in alphabetical order around the table. So, if I'm hosting the meeting and I'm not happy with our pound cake, everybody's got to bring a pound cake. I put my pound cake on the scale and explain why I'm not happy with it. We cut it. We taste it. We talk about what the selling price is and so forth. Then the next person puts his on the scale. We cut it and we go around the table. After everyone goes, we go to dinner. I don't know of anything that's ever happened to me that's more valuable than that group.

Then, in the early 1970s, there was an ingredient shortage. Prices for everything skyrocketed. A lot of bakeries went out of business, and Bennison's almost went under. To boost sales, they tried a concept store in the Central Street location.

"I knew a chef who had been with United Airlines," Guy said. "So, I made a deal with him. We had a setup where you could come in and buy a hot meal and take it out. That didn't catch on. We were ahead of our time. Eventually, it was a disaster."

Guy sold the equipment and closed the bakery on Central. They tried another café in their Wilmette bakery, but that didn't work out either. Slowly all the other shops closed, and Bennison's began to operate solely out of the Davis Street location, expanding that spot into a three-storefront location as neighboring businesses closed. The bakery reached its current size in 2012.

Over the years, Bennison's has gained notoriety in Chicago and the suburbs, not just for its baked goods—which include croissants, tortes, strudels, cakes, cookies, bread, rolls, stollen and more—but also for its service to the community. It hosts a pączki-eating contest annually as a fundraiser and works with local schools.

Bennison's is one of only a handful of bakeries in the Chicagoland area known for baumkuchen, a German tree cake. Jory special ordered an oven for it in the 1980s and had to pick it up in Germany. It is also one of the few spots to make atomic cake on the north side.

"I'll tell you a funny story about atomic torte," Guy said. "My wife, Jory's mother, was in the store, and she was talking to some Japanese customers. She was trying to sell them an atomic torte. They just wouldn't buy. So, when

Jory Downer slicing baumkuchen, a German tree cake. *Bennison's Bakery.*

they left, she said, 'I don't know why I couldn't sell it.' I told her, 'Think about it a little bit.' She just laughed."

Today, five of the recipes are still original to the first bakery: the pumpkin pie, the brownies, the fudge icing, the chocolate chip cookies and the September-only English rock cookies. Jory owns the bakery now. He's a member of the Bakers Dozen and plans to never retire.

CALUMET BAKERY

2510 East 106th Street in South Deering

Calumet Bakery is one of the few historic Chicago bakeries to occupy the same location since its opening. Instead of moving, Calumet expanded. The original shop, started by current owner Kerry Moore's grandfather in 1935, was—and still is—in South Deering. But there are also locations in Whiting, Indiana, and Lansing, Illinois.

Many of the original recipes are still in use at the bakery: nut rolls (voted the best in Chicago), chocolate donuts, sweet rolls and pastries. Calumet is also known for cakes, particularly the atomic cake. There's a bit of a debate over whether the chocolate, strawberry, banana and whipped cream creation was invented here or at Liberty Bakery.

"I was told that, in the '50s, this guy named Frank or George, who worked part time for my grandfather, came up with it," Moore once said. "He left to open Liberty Bakery in Roseland, but that's closed."

The cake debuted decades after Calumet opened, but perhaps we have both bakeries to thank for the enduring dessert.

WOLF'S BAKERY

3241 95th Street in Evergreen Park

Anyone who has ever attended the annual Fourth of July parade in Evergreen Park should recognize this familiar chant: "Lemon Fluff! Lemon Fluff! Can't get enough of Lemon Fluff!" The slogan is shouted from a float that looks like a tiered wedding cake in honor of Wolf's Bakery's best-seller, the Lemon

Fluff cake. It's a light-as-air lemon chiffon cake, filled and iced with whipped custard. The cake has been the signature item at the bakery since it opened and is still made using the original recipe.

Wolf's Bakery opened in June 1939. The original owners were Andy and Laurel Wolf, who opened the neighborhood spot about a block away from its current location. The couple opened two more locations, one at 103rd and Kedzie and another on 95th Street and a short-lived third shop around 111th and Western. Sadly, Andy died in the 1950s—leaving Laurel with three bakeries to run and two little girls to raise.

"She had to sink or swim," said Wolf's current owner, Pam, who requested her last name not be used for privacy reasons. "Women weren't allowed to run businesses then, and she had to go before a judge and prove she was of sound mind to operate the bakeries."

Current head baker Joe Boehm said that men in the bakery business were bullying Laurel, trying to get her to sell the bakery to them. But she never did, and "now we're still standing thanks to her," Pam said.

Boehm remembers working directly for Laurel. "I applied here out of high school, and I'm still here forty-four years later," he said. "My favorite memory is the day I started working here. I walked in and talked to Mrs. Wolf. She said, 'It isn't easy. There are no football games on the weekend, no dancing.' She asked if I could start right now and I said yes." He spent the rest of the day on his knees cleaning the floors—wearing his good clothes the entire time. By the time he got home, his clothes were covered in flour.

When Laurel was seventy-two, she decided to retire. She just wasn't having fun anymore. Pam and her husband bought it then, with the caveat that they couldn't fire any of the long-term employees. Boehm's mother was managing the bakery at that point and had worked there for thirty years.

Many of the old recipes moved forward along with the bakery, including the donuts, danishes, sweet rolls, Irish soda bread, cinnamon cylinder bread, atomic cakes, dinner rolls, tea cookies and muffins. But a newer recipe has helped the bakery gain a bit of fame in recent years: a copycat Dressel's whipped cream cake. Bakeries had been trying to duplicate the famed cake since Dressel's closed in the 1980s. One of the bakers at Wolf's, Dan, worked for Dressel's and knew how the cake was put together, so the team began testing out different recipes. Older customers came in to try the creations, and they did a process of elimination to get the right cake. They got close enough to the original cake that members of the Dressel family actually came to Wolf's to compliment the cake—though they noted the recipe wasn't *quite* there. In fact, they liked the cake so much that they gave Wolf's the original chemical formulas for the cake. Now, it's the second-best seller, behind only the lemon fluff cake.

Customers at Wolf's are extremely loyal and have been coming in for generations. What they buy can depend on the time of year. For St. Patrick's Day, they come in to get Irish soda bread. It's an award-winning recipe, and the bakery goes through about 2,000 loaves a week around the holiday. Easter sees hefty sales of lamb cakes. On Pączki Day, Wolf's sells 1,300 dozen pączki for just that day.

"You have to have so much adrenaline going, trying to make everything," Pam said. "I'm always so impressed with the holiday crew."

As for the future of the bakery? It's going to stick around. Pam has no intention to close, and Boehm doesn't plan to leave. "I want to be the oldest and the best baker on 95th Street," he said.

AUGUSTA BAKERY

901 North Ashland Avenue in Noble Square

Open as early as the 1940s and possibly earlier, Leonard Madoch's Augusta Bakery was famous for its seeded rye bread, sold both in the bakery and in local stores. It was made with sourdough, and the finished product was perfectly crusty, wrapped in a paper sleeve for sale. People drove in from other states just to get their hands on it. The cream cheese coffeecake was also popular, selling out by early afternoon daily. A full cake was about three feet long and eight inches wide, with a sweet yeast dough braided over a stuffing of sweet cheese and a few raisins. The top got an egg wash and coarse sugar that melted into a crust in the oven.

Eventually, Leonard retired, handing Augusta down to his son Lawrence. From there, the last few years of Augusta Bakery's existence were mostly spent in conflict. First, in 1986, Immigration and Naturalization Services raided the bakery based on an anonymous tip, arresting twelve employees—all legal immigrants from Poland, though working in the United States without permission. One of them, Pieka Ldzislaw, voluntarily returned to Poland within thirty days. The other eleven were deported. Then, in 1989, the bakery was battled over in divorce court. The last straw was in the early 1990s, when a court ruling sided with workers who had gone on strike several years earlier. The ongoing labor dispute caused the bakery to close.

MRS. HACKEL'S BAKERY

8560 South Chicago Avenue in South Chicago

On Saturday nights in the 1960s, Mrs. Hackel's Bakery was the place to be. Piping hot donuts and rolls churned off the conveyor belt, and anybody could go in to watch, learn how to frost chocolate donuts and enjoy the scent. Saturday night donuts became a tradition for local families, who were also able to buy the treats right off the belt. Weekends weren't the only evenings to stop by the bakery, though; after the bars closed in the wee morning hours, you could go buy freshly baked rolls from the bakery's back door.

Sweet smells regularly drifted down the block from the bakery, pulling customers in to try the much-loved donuts and rolls, plus bismarcks, poppy seed buns, sweet peanut rolls, long johns, bread and cinnamon rolls. The pastries were so popular that families returned weekly for generations.

Children were cherished at Mrs. Hackel's Bakery. She was a Girl Scout leader outside the bakery, and when kids stopped in, they were treated like royalty. They'd get little handfuls of raw dough to play with and bake at home; the bakers would pull a fresh donut off the tray and give it to children for free every now and then; and if you were really lucky, they let you frost it yourself.

Mrs. Hackel's Bakery was acquired by Dressel's in 1964.

HOEFFKEN'S THE BUSY BAKERY

3044 West 63rd Street in Chicago Lawn

Raymond Hoeffken was a legendary German baker in Chicago. He was a mentor to many and a friend to all during the time he operated his Busy Bakery, from 1940 to 1985. Even today, Chicago bakers fondly remember Hoeffken as one of the best.

But Hoeffken's legacy—and his recipes—live on in a surprising place: a donut shop in Jackson, Mississippi. The owner, Monroe Jackson, started working at The Busy Bakery in the early 1970s. He'd left work in the cottonfields in Lexington, Mississippi, to find a job in Chicago in 1972.

"I always say my life is full of 'God moments,' and this really was one of them," Jackson later said. "I'd never bought a newspaper in my life until that day. I sat down and started looking at all the jobs listed in there."

Mike Weber of Weber's Bakery on Hoeffken's Urban Legend

Hoeffken owned the South Side. He ran a business that was just unbelievable. In fact, he had so many bakers working at one point, that there's a story about it. I don't know if it's true but it's definitely an urban legend. Two guys were working on a bench and one guy kept getting close to the other guy, so he dusted some flour and made a line. He said, "Don't cross the line." And the guy did. So the baker that made the line took the rolling pin he was working with and he hit the other baker and broke four fingers. And he said, "I said don't cross the line."

One of those jobs was The Busy Bakery, looking for a porter—a glorified term for a dishwasher. Jackson stopped in the next morning to apply, and at first Hoeffken didn't want to hire him. He needed somebody big and strong enough to handle all the heavy equipment, and Jackson was just a teenager. But Jackson didn't take no for an answer and told Hoeffken to try him for a week. If he wasn't satisfied, Jackson would leave and not accept any pay for the job he did. Hoeffken ended up keeping Jackson on staff. The baker took Jackson under his wing, and within four months, he promoted him to the kitchen.

This was a time in Chicago when racism was firmly and outwardly entrenched in the community. White men threw glass bottles at Jackson as he waited for the bus near the bakery. All twelve bakers inside The Busy Bakery were white and actively opposed Hoeffken promoting Jackson to baker. They tried to sabotage his recipes. But Hoeffken didn't fall for it and taught Jackson everything he needed to know about running a bakery.

"He treated me better than my own father," Jackson later recalled.

Hoeffken died in 1987, and Jackson was so distressed that he vowed to never bake again. He worked as a butcher for a few months, and then he and his wife (Cindy, whom he met while working at the bakery) moved to Mississippi. Before they left, he gathered the items Hoeffken left for him in his will: every recipe from the bakery.

Hoeffken knew something Jackson didn't—once a baker, always a baker. Seven years after moving to Mississippi, Jackson opened his own bakery, Monroe's Donuts and Bakery, with the goal of keeping Hoeffken's dream and vision alive.

"That man taught me way more than how to bake things," Jackson later said. "He taught me that friendship and love have nothing to do with a person's color. It's about the person's heart. And Mr. Hoeffken had the biggest heart I've ever known."

BRIDGEPORT BAKERY

2907 South Archer Avenue in Bridgeport

Depending on who you ask, Bridgeport Bakery (now Bridgeport Bakery 2.0) has been open for either about fifty years or about eighty years. It was first a Polish bakery, opened by Frank and Virginia Michalski in 1941. They owned it until 1975. After that, Ron Pavelka took over—he learned to bake and to run a bakery from the Michalskis. He ran Bridgeport until 2019. The notice posted online and in the bakery when he retired said it was closing after forty-seven years, but even Pavelka's staff couldn't remember what year they took over. And news articles swap the years back and forth with regularity.

Regardless, Bridgeport Bakery is a staple in the community—and so are the pączki, bacon buns (a Lithuanian specialty, a soft bun stuffed with bacon and onions) and kolache. When Pavelka decided to close, the community was in mourning. Customers were crying in the streets. They lined the block around the bakery beginning at 5:00 a.m. the last day, which wasn't anything unusual. But by 9:00 a.m., the bakery was sold out of virtually everything.

Even though Bridgeport Bakery was still immensely popular, Pavelka needed to quit. He had quadruple bypass surgery and was under strict advice from his doctor to relax. His sister, Sandy Budz, worked the front of the store and baked, and she decided to retire alongside her brother. So did baker Barbara Betourney and some of the other staff.

For a rough few months, no one was planning to pick up the reins of the bakery and keep it in business. Then came Can Lao. Lao, a Chinese immigrant and Bridgeport resident for twenty years, stepped up to buy the bakery in 2020. He became Pavelka's apprentice, learning all the recipes the bakery was known for—even though he'd never professionally baked. Before taking over, Lao was a pharmacist.

"Bridgeport Bakery is my pastry school, kind of…I learned from the best," Lao said in 2020. Lao renamed the bakery Bridgeport Bakery 2.0; updated just the flooring and the lighting ("I wanted to keep the old look," he said); hired back many of the previous staff; and turned back on the red neon "Bridgeport Bakery" sign. Customers took notice immediately, again lining up around the block. At Lao's soft opening, bacon buns sold out by 6:00 a.m.

"I'm from Bridgeport, and a lot of people were so sad when this closed," Lao said at the time. "I wasn't expecting that much support from the customers. [They'd say] 'Oh my God, you're open?' and they keep giving suggestions."

Those suggestions have both helped Lao perfect the recipes and encouraged him to expand the menu. He now carries cannoli, shumai, BBQ pork buns, dim sum, Mexican concha and some other ethnic specialties.

"I get feedback from the customers," Lao said. "I ask them, did this taste the same, did it taste different compared to before, what do you like. A lot of people message me if I do something wrong or good. Those are little things I try to learn. I ask a lot of questions. I tell the bakers the feedback and figure out how we can fix things and make things better. We just keep evolving."

BEIL'S BAKERY

4229 West Montrose Avenue in Mayfair

After three generations of operation, Beil's Bakery moved out of Chicago in 1999. It was a hard pill to swallow for many customers whose families had been visiting the bakery since 1943—and a difficult decision for the owners, Eleanor and William Beil, to make.

William's father, Mathias, opened the bakery after immigrating to Chicago from Germany. At that time, bakeries made everything from scratch, starting the night before or getting up at dawn to get the ovens roaring.

"It's all shortcuts today, everything in terms of it has to be done quick," William said in 1999. "Most bakers open up a bucket from a supplier and smear [buttercream] on a cake. To me, it's robotic. A robot can't tell how something tastes. We can tell. The only way to stop that is to stay small enough so you can do it right."

The Beils had few options: increase their workload, which was already at about seventy hours a week; lower their standards and stop making everything from scratch; or close. They tried to stay open, searching for bakers both in the United States and in Germany to come in and learn the recipes. But no one surfaced, and at the height of the business with lines still stretching down the block, they decided to shut down. Everyone mourned the loss: customers, employees and owners alike. Eleanor and William had been a fixture in Mayfair, spending time with community members, joining the local German American choir and even once serving as witnesses in a murder trial.

But there was a bit of hope still. Eleanor and William's son, Carl, decided he would open a smaller location up in Delavan, Wisconsin. That bakery opened in 1999, supplying new locals and a steady stream of visiting Chicagoans with the brownies, coffeecakes, beinenstich, cookies and bread that made them famous. Carl and his wife, Beth, retired and closed the Delavan shop in 2016.

PTICEK AND SON

5523 South Narragansett Avenue in Garfield Ridge

In 1943, John Pticek and his wife, Antionette, opened Pticek and Son Bakery at 1925 South Racine Avenue. Pticek came to the United States from Croatia when he was twelve to join his father, who was already in Chicago. He was broke, except for one thing: a silver half dollar he found on the ship. Pticek carried that half dollar with him until the day he died.

"He came on the ship *America*," said his daughter, Toni DeWitt, who owns the bakery now. "He found that fifty-cent piece and I don't know where it is, but it's still hidden somewhere. He was always lucky, but he was a hard worker, too."

Sadly, six months after Pticek arrived in the States, his dad died in an accident. Pticek was sent downstate for a few years but returned to Chicago when he turned sixteen. First he worked in a candy factory, and then he moved to a bakery. He loved it so much that he bought his first bakery—the one on Racine Avenue—when he was twenty-eight. After about ten years, he and his wife moved the shop to a custom-built bakery on Narragansett Avenue, where the shop still is today.

The entire family worked in the bakery over the years. Antionette managed the store; their son, Michael, was in charge of production and their daughter, Toni, decorated cakes and took orders. Toni's daughter, Antionette Wingo, worked at the counter, and Toni's son Joseph baked. The elder Antionette wouldn't allow the girls to wear pants in the store—it was white dresses only. Toni and her daughter carry on that tradition today.

Toni DeWitt on the Eating Habits of a Baker

One time my husband and I were over in Hawaii, and I said, "Okay, we've got to stop at a bakery." And he goes, "Are you kidding me?" And I said, "I have to have bakery." I was born and raised in it. And he goes, "Aren't you tired of it?" Nope, nope, I love my bakery. I've got to have bakery wherever we go. I'm like my dad, I can taste if something is missing.

The sign outside Pticek and Son Bakery. *Author's collection.*

Pticek and Son quickly gained a loyal following, thanks to the variety of food and the quality of ingredients. Some of the favorite items (that are still around today) are the Croatian walnut cake, cinnamon bread, almond horns, cheese-filled coffeecakes, donuts, sour cream cheesecakes and kolaches. That rich flavor you taste when you bite into anything from the shop is thanks to from-scratch processes with no substitutions for real ingredients.

"My dad always said the only thing better than butter is more butter," Toni said. "When margarine came out, he said no, I'm not going to use it. A lot of bakers went to it, but he didn't. So, everything is handmade right here."

The bakery goes through more than 450 pounds of real butter every week. Toni wakes up at 3:30 every morning to get to work decorating cakes and desserts. They need to fill up the showcases by the time Pticek and Son opens at 5:15 a.m.

"I always wondered why my parents went to bed so early," Toni said. "Now I know."

The Icing on the Cake

The author's great-grandmother used to frequent Pticek and Son.

ALLEGRETTI'S BAKERY

7717 West Lawrence Avenue in Norridge

Allegretti's Bakery may be in suburban Norridge, but it has roots in Chicago. Anthony Allegretti was a cook in the U.S. Army during World War II. When he came home in 1947, he took up a baking side gig in his uncle's basement in Chicago, putting out birthday cakes and small wedding cakes. He got pretty good at it, too—enough to be considered competition by a local bakery. So, the owners at Sarno's Pastry Shop offered Allegretti a job. He said no, though; he wanted to keep up what he was doing on his own terms.

A few years later, in 1952, the owners at Sarno's decided to retire. This time, they approached Allegretti with a new proposal. "You didn't want to work for us," they said, "but will you buy the entire bakery?" He said yes and moved his business into the Sarno's shop in Little Italy. Eventually, he moved his family—wife Rose and five children—into the apartment above the bakery. In 1960, they changed the name Sarno's to Allegretti's and moved the bakery to Park Ridge. Linda Ahern, Allegretti's daughter, who runs the

A window display of lamb cakes and Easter bread at Sarno's Pastry Shop after Anthony Allegretti took over. *Allegretti's Bakery.*

The current storefront of Allegretti's Bakery. *Author's collection.*

business now with her brother, said the Park Ridge location was a disaster. There wasn't enough Italian clientele for an Italian bakery to work. So they "limped along" for two years, she said, before moving into the bakery's current spot in Norridge in 1962.

Along the way, Allegretti's gained fame for enormous wedding cakes. Like Ferrara, the bakery made cakes for peanut weddings. The cakes were so tall that Anthony would have to climb a ladder to cut it, and flanking the cake on both sides were smaller treat towers filled with castagnoles. Allegretti got so good at making wedding cakes that he started to put a little extra showmanship into it.

"He was one of the first people to put a fountain in the center of a cake," Ahern said. "One cake, he had it set up, and when everybody was standing around it going, this is really pretty, he flipped a switch in the back. Lights came on up top, a fountain in the cake started to run, and at the bottom, the cake rotated. After that, nobody looked at the bride the whole night."

He also used to play a good-natured trick on the marrying couples. He'd tell them to take the top layer of their cake and freeze it, since it was tradition to eat the top layer on your first anniversary. If they brought it back in to the bakery for their first anniversary, he said he would redecorate it so it looked good as new.

"So they would bring it in, and I'd ask them to give us about an hour or so," Ahern said. "They'd come back, and we would give them their cake all decorated. Then, they'd come back in the next day or two and say, 'I have to tell you, that cake was as good as the day we first had it.' And that's because it was. My father would make them a whole new cake. He'd say, 'Nothing is good in the freezer for a year.' And they were always so amazed."

It wasn't always easy, though, to tell what the cake and its filling actually were—it had been sitting in the freezer for a year, after all. Ahern got clever about it. When they'd bring in the cake, she'd ask them to relive their memories of the wedding and what their cake was in order to get the right combination for her dad to re-create.

Large wedding cakes eventually went out of style, but Allegretti's had plenty of other treats to keep business going strong. Think classic Italian cookies, filled-as-you-order cannoli, sfogliatelle, pasticiotto, baba rum and the signature items: the chocolate donuts and the chocolate-frosted pound cake. On the holidays, the bakery did a brisk business of lamb cakes, gingerbread houses and casatiello. But nothing beats Allegretti's zeppole. They were featured on Chicago's Best one year, and the bakery was completely swarmed.

Trays of Allegretti's Bakery castagnole lined up on a table for a traditional Italian American peanut wedding. *Allegretti's Bakery.*

> Linda Ahern on the Generosity of Her Father, Anthony Allegretti
>
> I remember the day of the 1967 blizzard, my dad couldn't get the car out, but he walked to the bakery. He made bread, and anybody who came in, he gave them a loaf. But my all-time favorite thing was after a holiday when my dad was alive. We'd be bone-tired from working the few days beforehand. My mother would be waiting at home for us to come for dinner. But my father had me pack up almost everything that was left over. We stopped at the convent and brought them stuff, we stopped at the rectory, the fire house and the police station. Every holiday he did that. He was such a generous person.

"I told them, you can do an article, you can do a feature," Ahern said. "But you can't air it until the night of St. Joseph's Day. We can't have it run beforehand because we can't handle the customers we have now."

Of course, they aired it before St. Joseph's Day anyway.

"I came in, my sister came in, my cousins came in, and a girlfriend of mine came in, just to help the regular staff," Ahern said. "People were lined up down the block and around the corner. There was still a line at 6:00 when we closed."

All the zeppole the bakery sells are handmade, and come 6:00 p.m., the team just couldn't do anymore; their hands hurt too bad. So Ahern took business cards and signed her name on them. She went out to everyone still standing in line and told them if they came back the next day, she'd give them extra. Buy a half dozen, you get a dozen. Buy a dozen, you get two dozen.

"I was thinking, 'Today is St. Joseph's Day. Who's coming in tomorrow? We opened that door at 7:00 a.m. and the line was out the door," Ahern said.

By that point, Ahern and her brother Mike Allegretti were already running the business with their siblings. Anthony died suddenly in 1973 from a heart attack. The bakery closed for six weeks as the family determined how to move forward. A number of people offered to buy the business, but they wanted to purchase the name, too—and Rose wouldn't allow it. When the doors reopened, it was under the leadership of Ahern and Michael.

"The day my dad died, he made a batch of sfogliatelle," Ahern said. "It's a two-day project, and he had worked all day on it. So the next day, when I came to put the sign on the door, I looked in the refrigerator and saw they were sitting in there. He had planned to bake them off. I put them in a bag, brought them home, and put them in my freezer. Ten years later, I threw them out. I couldn't part with them; they were the last thing he touched."

Transitioning the bakery to Ahern and Michael wasn't the easiest. Apparently, Anthony had left an ingredient or two out of every recipe he'd used, and the siblings had to use trial and error to get everything to how it used to be. Today, all the recipes are still the same as they were when Allegretti's first opened. The next generation of ownership, Ahern's nephew, is in training to take over the business.

BOB'S SUGAR BOWL

11208 South St. Lawrence Avenue in Pullman

For decades, Bob's Sugar Bowl was the only place to grab something sweet in the Pullman neighborhood on the far south side. But it wasn't the first. The building was originally built to be a bakery in 1916, across from the Greenstone Church, serving residents in what was a recently failed company town for Pullman train cars. The owner was Joseph Guest, an immigrant from Dublin, Ireland. He moved to Pullman in 1910 and took a job working as the chef and manager at the Pullman Executive's Club. While working there, he lived behind the club. But in 1912, he bought a home in Pullman proper and then built the bakery next door a few years later.

Pullman Bakery in 1916 with a delivery truck and the owner Joseph Guest standing outside. *Illinois Digital Archive.*

Outside Bob's Sugar Bowl in Pullman. *Illinois Digital Archive.*

After the original bakery closed, the building housed a candy shop, a butcher, a laundry run by Chinese immigrants and a boat shop. Bob Dournas opened the Sugar Bowl in 1947. Bob lived upstairs and eventually ran the business with his daughter. Kids loved the shop—they'd stop in for Green River pop, burgers and sweet snacks. When Bob's closed, the neighborhood faced a tremendous and long-lasting loss.

The Pullman Café coffeeshop opened in this spot in 2015. It was a long time coming for a neighborhood that hadn't had a café, coffeeshop or eatery since Bob's closed. Bob's Sugar Bowl was closed by 2005, replaced in 2007 with a resale shop called Dig It! Pullman. It was open for only two years and then replaced by a short-lived tax preparation office. After that office closed, local artist Ian Lantz dreamed of opening a café and coffeeshop in the former soda fountain space. Lantz was already locally famous for painting colorful murals on garage doors in Pullman alleys. Now he's famous again for bringing a much-needed eatery back to the neighborhood. And the neighborhood had a big hand in bringing the café to fruition, too. The antique church pews inside were donated by the Historic Pullman Foundation, the wood furniture was handmade by Lantz's family and then it was painted by Method soap employees, who worked at a factory near the historic district.

HECK'S BAKERY

2038 West Roscoe Street in Roscoe Village

Ask anyone what they remember about Heck's Bakery the most, and they'll likely tell you about the coffeecake. It was a dense and thick streusel square, about a foot long on each side. There was a ring in the middle that was stuffed with custard, and then the entire thing was sprinkled with pecans and iced. When Heck's closed in 1983, the community worried they'd never see that coffeecake again—but fate was on their side.

Edna and Ernest Heck opened Heck's Bakery in 1947. While Ernest baked all the treats, Edna worked the counter and ran the store. Aside from the coffeecake, they were known for chocolate donuts, rum balls, chocolate chip cookies, sweet rolls, fruit slices, layer cakes and an assortment of other coffeecakes, like chocolate chip and cheese pizza flavors. Edna was known around the neighborhood for being generous with her time and baked goods, contributing to various fundraisers.

"She had a real big heart," her daughter Carol Wilkinson said when Edna passed in April 2000. "She always wanted to help."

The Hecks left Roscoe Village in 1983, when they sold the bakery and retired to the suburbs. Another bakery took Heck's spot, and hope for the coffeecake faded.

But then Rudy came along. Rudy was a baker at Heck's, and when the bakery closed, he bought some of the recipes—including the coffeecake. The second bakery in the spot closed, and Rudy now runs Rudy's Bakery there. Many of the old recipes from Heck's are on the menu, and the beloved coffeecake is known as the Heck's Special.

LUTZ CAFÉ AND PASTRY SHOP

2458 West Montrose Avenue in Ravenswood

In the world of German baking in Chicago, there's one cake to rule them all: baumkuchen. It translates to "tree cake," a moniker that makes sense once you get a look at it. The cake stands up to three feet tall, bulging out in parallel sections. The bulges are thanks to how it's made: on a spit spinning over an oven. Layer after layer of crepe-thin batter is piled onto the spit in

Lutz Café and Pastry Shop in 1977. *Library of Congress.*

A window display at Lutz Café and Pastry Shop in 1977. *Library of Congress.*

sections, making a long, continuous cake with an undulating exterior. The layers form thin rings inside, so when you cut into it, it looks like a slice of ancient tree trunk.

Lutz Café and Pastry Shop is famous for its baumkuchen. It's one of the few bakeries remaining in the city with an actual operating spit to make the cake. The finished product is mildly sweet with an almond essence and pairs perfectly with coffee or tea. Lutz's baumkuchen was once featured on the Food Network, and overnight, the bakery received several hundred orders for the German delight.

That recipe—and many of the others—came from Germany along with the original owner when it opened in 1948. The shop is technically a *konditorei*, the German term for a pastry and coffee shop. It's scaled back some from the original iteration, though, when there was a full menu, a well-appointed dining room, an outdoor tea garden and waitresses clad in dresses with white aprons. But that atmosphere remains, as do all the delicious pastries, including tortes, cookies, strudel, chocolates, stollen, marzipan and bienenstich.

III

1950s to 1970s

From the 1950s to the 1970s, Chicago bakeries truly began to embrace the diversity of the city at large. They addressed their changing neighborhoods by creating not just the treats they knew how to make but also the ones locals were requesting that were a bit out of their comfort zone. And that shift catapulted food traditions to the entirety of the city.

Here, we begin to see bacon buns expand beyond neighborhood spots to become a loved part of South Side culture. We see pączki sales develop into full-blown Pączki Day (Fat Tuesday) celebrations, complete with novel fillings in the Polish treats—now being sold all over the city—and accordion players walking the long lines outside bakeries. Shops went from selling a few trays of pączki to selling tens of thousands on that one day alone. We also welcome the invention of the atomic cake, a treat found only on the south side and a staple at many family celebrations.

LIBERTY BAKERY

11932 South Halsted Street in Roseland

Liberty Bakery, owned by George Kremm and his wife, officially launched the atomic cake in the 1950s, around the time the bakery opened. George had the idea percolating for a while; he came up with it while working at

Calumet Bakery. The fruity whipped cream cake concoction wasn't all Liberty was known for, though. It also sold popular strudel, donuts, bread and wedding cakes.

JUERGEN'S NORTH STAR BAKERY

4545 North Lincoln Avenue in Lincoln Square

Juergen's North Star Bakery was a commercial bakery, but it was known around the city for its rye bread when the facility was open. The bestseller was North Star's kommissbrot, a dark bread made from a mixture of rye and wheat flours and sold in a round, chewy loaf. Visitors were welcome to come into the front of the bakery and buy a loaf from counters towering with fresh bread, but most of it left in trucks. About two thousand loaves were shipped daily throughout the United States. Juergen's North Star Bakery closed when the owner, James Meyer, retired in suburban Park Ridge.

SICILIAN BAKERY

4632 North Cumberland Avenue in Schorsch Forest View

In 1952, Silvio Gagliardi opened a bakery on Chicago Avenue. He had come to Chicago a few years before, first taking a job at Ferrara Bakery and then branching out on his own. Twenty years later, in 1972, Gagliardi's nephew Phil Rubino came to Chicago from Sicily. Rubino was only thirteen, but he knew one thing: he wanted to be a baker. He began working at his Uncle Silvio's bakery every day after school to learn the trade. Gagliardi died in 1977, but Rubino continued working at the bakery. In 1984, he officially took over the business.

Rubino moved the shop to Grand and Pulaski, opened a second store on Grand and Harlem and eventually moved completely to Cumberland Avenue, closing the other two stores. Over the years, the bakery gained more and more popularity—not just for its traditional Italian pastries like cannoli, lemon taralli and quaresimale, but also for its Sicilian-style pizza. The pizza

The sign at Sicilian Bakery's current storefront. *Author's collection.*

is on a thick, almost focaccia-like bread, covered in fresh tomato sauce and sprinkled with salt and cheese. It's regularly considered one of the best pizzas in Chicago.

Zeppole are also a big seller at Sicilian Bakery. They start making custard and cannoli zeppole for St. Joseph's Day beginning around Valentine's Day and continue making them through Easter. It's all made by hand, cooked over the stove and hand-piped into the deep fryer. The recipe is a family heirloom, passed down from Uncle Silvio. On St. Joseph's Day, the bakery sells up to five thousand zeppole.

Today, Phil runs the bakery with his son, Anthony. And Anthony has no intention to change the bakery once he takes over—whenever that might be.

"I'm next in line for the throne," he said. "My dad's not ready to retire, but he's slowing down. My plan is to keep it as-is. If it's not broken, why fix it? We thrive on the originality and quality of our product and people really appreciate that. We have a lot of older clients that have been regular customers for generations. Now, we're starting to see the kids and grandkids return, which makes us even happier and more grateful."

ALBANO'S BAKE SHOP

7816 West North Avenue in Elmwood Park

Though Albano's Bake Shop was in suburban Elmwood Park when it closed in 2015, the bakery first opened at the corner of Taylor and Western in Little Italy in 1953. The owner, Emilia Albano, was known as Grandma Albano to everyone in the neighborhood. When she wasn't making cannoli cakes for birthdays and weddings, Albano was handing out cookies to kids that stopped by or having young customers come in the back and help put cherries on desserts and fill cannoli.

"When I was a young kid, I'd walk in there with change in my pocket thinking it was a candy store and Mrs. Albano would give me a bag full

Albano's Bake Shop at 7816 West North Avenue in the 1950s. *Illinois Digital Archive.*

of cookies for a handful of coins, God bless her!" one former customer remembered.

Donuts and danishes were popular items for sale, as were the fresh-baked breads and a lemon cheesecake shaped like a loaf of bread. Albano's daughter, Frieda, also ran a bakery that sold many of these same goods.

The bakery had a dark side, though—Eugene Albano, Emilia's son, who eventually took over the bakery, was involved with the mob. Eugene's cousin was in the mafia, and he helped out mobster Paul Ricca on an almost daily basis, driving him to the track and placing bets for him. It got to the point where the FBI had a permanent surveillance car set up outside the bakery to monitor who came in and out when Eugene hosted card games.

That didn't stop loyal patrons from coming into the bakery, though. The cannoli were worth it.

"I remember the last box of cannoli that we bought from Albano, before they closed for good," one former customer recalled. "We all stood around eating them in silence, savoring every last bite, as if we were at a funeral. Which, kind of, we were."

EL NOPAL BAKERY

3648 West 26th Street in Little Village

For more than sixty years, El Nopal Bakery has been putting a lot of heart into baking. It shows in the cookies: heart-shaped cinnamon cookies called hojarascas that have been bestsellers from the beginning. They're delicate, sweet, slightly spiced and perfect with a cup of tea. And today, they're still made with the original recipe.

Francisco and Celia Bonilla first opened El Nopal in 1954 on the near west side. In the 1960s, they relocated to 1844 South Blue Island Avenue in Pilsen. The building dated to 1885 and first housed a bakery called Ace Bakery, run by the Fritz family. The Fritzes sold the building to the Bonillas. In 1974, they opened a second El Nopal location in Little Village.

The Pilsen building had a lot of memories built in by the time it closed in the 2010s. The bakery became known for its Mexican breads and pastries, like pan dulce, polvorones, bolillo bread, tres leches and those hojarascas—a creation of Celia's. The shop was featured in movies and music videos. Once, Francisco saw a building on fire across the street. He instantly went to knock on doors in the building to tell people to get out and ended up saving sixty-five lives in the process. El Nopal in Pilsen closed when Francisco and Celia passed away; Francisco had gotten sick and died, and Celia followed six months later. Their son Frank closed that location and moved all operations to the bakery in Little Village, where it still operates today—with one small lapse.

In 2015, Frank decided to retire and close down El Nopal. He put the business up for sale with the hopes that someone would come in, buy the space and the recipes and continue on his parents' legacy. He found that person in his friend and longtime customer Ozzie Ocegueda. Ocegueda bought the bakery, joined forces with Eugenio Vargas (a baker at El Nopal before it closed) and reopened in 2017. All the recipes are the same, and Ocegueda has since hired on a second baker who worked there before its closure. The first day they were open, they sold more than three hundred boxes of hojarascas.

"People come in and say our cookies taste exactly like they did sixty years ago," Ocegueda said. "We try to keep the tradition going."

Ocegueda's wife is the pastry chef at the bakery and is there full time while he works a second job as a chef. He likes to join her in the afternoons, though, because that's when customers come in to share their memories, he said.

The sign at El Nopal Bakery's current storefront. *Author's collection.*

Treats on display inside El Nopal Bakery. *Author's collection.*

"I've heard so many stories about not just the bakery but the community," Ocegueda said. "Customers tell us their parents used to bring them in, and now they bring in their grandkids. It's so nice to hear that. One of my favorite stories is when a lot of people would come in on Sundays, and Mr. Bonilla would hand them a cookie and talk to them. He used to make an alligator bread, a big bread in the form of an alligator. He'd put it out front and cut it up and just let everybody have it."

Ocegueda has no plans to slow down. They own another full-size space next to El Nopal, which they want to expand into a fried chicken concept. He also has plans to bring in some coffee to the bakery from Dark Matter Coffee. It just opened in the former El Nopal location in Pilsen and sells the bakery's bread. Ocegueda wants to return the favor. But regardless of the changes, he says, "We want to keep the bakery the same."

GROVES BAKERY

5355 West North Avenue in Austin

In the '60s and '70s, Groves Bakery supplied the Austin neighborhood with a full supply of cookies, cakes, sweet rolls, Easter lamb cakes, butter-crust buns and coffeecakes. Joseph Groves opened the shop with his wife, Mary, sometime after World War II. He was a Pearl Harbor survivor. Neighborhood kids loved stopping into the shop because they always left with a free cookie. After the Groves moved to Florida in 1986, their bakery became Curlie's Bakery, which is now closed.

STEFFENS BAKERY

714 State Line Road in Calumet City

Steffens Bakery, owned by Paul Steffens, wasn't always just outside the city limits. At one time, it was located at 83rd Place and Stoney Island, in the Stoney Island Park neighborhood. Regardless of where it was located, though, customers and neighbors have many fond memories of the shop—everything from enjoying the smell of baking donuts wafting down the street at 4:00 a.m. every day to spontaneously decorating cakes with an employee after school.

Steffens opened his bakery in the 1960s, running the shop with his wife, Joan. They were known for delicious butter cookies, brownies, atomic cakes and pączki. Steffens used to sell about 750 dozen pączki on Pączki Day alone. The donuts were equally memorable; one past customer shared that they ordered the donuts for a reunion, and some of the attendees cried when they took that first bite. It transported them back to childhood so intensely that the emotions just poured out.

Paul and Joan entered a quasi-retirement in 2011, continuing to open for one-day-only sales for a few years. The special sales included items like pączki, lamb cakes and atomic cakes by special order. In 2014, a new bakery, Cal City Bakery, opened in Steffens's location. Paul died in 2017.

TURANO BAKING CO.

6501 Roosevelt Road in Berwyn

In 1962, recent Italian immigrant Mariano Turano spent $200 on an oven and opened a six-hundred-square-foot bakery. He named the business Campagna Bakery. Turano's dream was to provide a better life for his family, so he kicked off the bakery with something he had a hunch would sell: an old-fashioned Italian round bread made with his great-grandfather's recipe. Turano was right. He baked the bread while his wife, Assunta, ran the store, and soon people were clamoring for loaves. Three years later, in 1965, Turano joined forces with his brothers, Carmen and Eugenio, and formed Campagna-Turano Bakery in Berwyn.

Even more success was on the way. The brothers expanded the menu in 1967, introducing more bread styles: French bread, Vienna bread and kaiser rolls. They also launched a pizza line called Mamma Susi's pizza; Assunta made them in the bakery, and locals fell in love. Soon, the company was supplying bread and pizza to local restaurants and grocery stores.

Mamma Susi's pizzas were groundbreaking in Chicago. They were the first mass-produced frozen pizzas in the area that you could buy in a grocery store. It was a simple recipe: bread, a light tomato sauce and cheese. Sales immediately skyrocketed, to the point where the bakery couldn't keep up with the orders. By the mid-1970s, pizza production had stopped.

A Turano Baking Company delivery truck. *Creative Commons.*

Eventually, Turano passed the business to his three sons, Renato, Umberto and Giancarlo. They officially renamed the bakery Turano Baking Company and created partnerships around the country, allowing them to open more bakeries—another in Illinois, one in Georgia, one in Florida and one in Nevada. The original bakery became a small bakeshop attached to the larger facility.

In 2008, thanks to Assunta's granddaughter Renee, Mamma Susi's pizzas made a comeback. The original bakery space was renamed Mamma Susi's Bakeshop. Renee and her cousin Jennifer pulled out Assunta's old oven and her old recipe and set to work producing the pizzas once more.

"It's unbelievable how many people walk in and say, 'Oh my god, Mamma Susi pizza!'" Renee said at the time, describing the emotional process of bringing the bakery back to its roots. "It reminds me of where we started in 1962. I have a whole new respect for my parents, uncles and grandparents."

The pizzas are still for sale in the bakeshop, along with cannoli, eclairs, Italian cookies, tiramisu, and other specialties. As for the bread, that's on sale in the shop as well and also supplied throughout the Midwest. Turano now makes more than four hundred breads and baked goods.

FROM TURANO'S RECIPE BOX

Mamma Susi's Pizza (from Turano's website)

Mamma Susi Pizza is named in honor of our family's grandmother Assunta. It is a traditional Calabrese focaccia, which is a flavorful dough topped with "pomodori" (tomatoes) and various cheeses. It is reminiscent of the homemade pizza "Nonna" (grandma) used to bake almost daily.
Yield: About 20 slices

Dough Ingredients
2 cups warm water, about 105 degrees
2½ tablespoons extra virgin olive oil, plus 2 tablespoons for greasing pan
½ ounce dry yeast
1¾ pounds all-purpose flour, plus extra for rolling out dough
¾ ounce salt
Cornmeal or flour for dusting pan

Pizza Ingredients
9 to 10 Roma plum tomatoes, sliced
1 pound fresh mozzarella, thinly sliced
1 cup fresh basil leaves, thinly sliced
Kosher salt

Directions
In a 4- or 5-quart bowl, combine water, olive oil and yeast. Allow to ferment for five minutes. Add yeast water to the flour and salt, then mix on medium speed for about five minutes, or until the dough is elastic. If dough is too wet, add flour a little at a time until moist, but not too sticky. Remove from mixer and cover tightly. Place in a warm spot and allow to double in size, about 30 minutes.

Preheat oven to 350. Brush an 11¾-by-16½-inch sheet pan with olive oil; dust with cornmeal. Roll out dough on floured surface to ½-inch thick, transfer to sheet pan, allow to raise for another 15 minutes, then dot surface with a fork.

Bake on center rack for about 8 minutes or until slightly browned. Remove from oven. Arrange sliced tomatoes to cover entire surface and add slices of fresh mozzarella, layered slightly under tomato slices. Return pizza to oven. Continue to bake until cheese melts and begins to brown around the edges. Remove from oven, allowing to cool slightly, then sprinkle with basil leaves and salt to taste.

VIENNA PASTRY SHOP

5411 West Addison Street in Portage Park

By the time Vienna Pastry Shop opened in Chicago, it was already a second-generation business. Gerhard Kaes and his wife, Hedwig, ran a shop of the same name (opened by Gerhard's parents) in Vienna, Austria. That bakery was destroyed by bombs during World War II.

After the war, Gerhard and Hedwig moved to Chicago. They opened the new shop in 1964 as one of the only authentic Austrian bakeries in the city. Menu items reflected that heritage; they sold faschingskrapfen; apple and cherry strudel; windbäckerei; linzer, sacher and dobosh tortes; and preßburger mohnstrudel, made with poppy seeds and walnuts.

Tragedy struck the business in 1999. Johann Kaes, Gerhard and Hedwig's son and the head baker at the shop, was killed in a car accident. He was just thirty-one years old.

"You never really expect this," his sister Gabriella said at the time. "I expected to have him forever."

The bakery abruptly closed a few years later.

LAPETITE PASTRY

5610 West 63rd Street in Clearing

LaPetite Pastry is a true multicultural business. Owner Bill Goebel was born and raised in Germany, and he studied to be a baker under some of the best bakers in the country. When he turned seventeen, he came to Chicago

The sign at LaPetite Pastry's current location. *Author's collection.*

to work in his uncle Kurt Bunde's shop. After working there for a bit, Bill moved to Haas Bakery. He worked there until he left for a stint in the army.

Three years later, Bill was back in Chicago and back at Haas. He worked there until 1967, when Charlie Haas offered him the chance to buy a small bakery in an Irish neighborhood. LaPetite Pastry was born. So now there was a French bakery in an Irish neighborhood owned by a German baker.

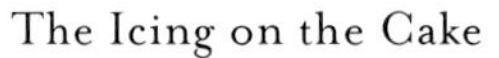

> The Icing on the Cake
>
> The author's mother used to frequent LaPetite Pastry. Her mother gave her bus fare for school, but instead of taking the bus, she'd use the money to buy cream-filled chocolate cupcakes at the bakery and walk to school.

The bakery moved to a new location in 1972. Bill's future wife, Kim, was working as the assistant manager there when Bill suggested she manage a second shop. She said yes, and they bought a new building (a former bakery) in 1982. The 1972 location closed in 1998, and they've been in the current spot with Bill and Kim at the helm ever since. The location works really well—it's the closest bakery to Midway International Airport, as in, right across the street.

LaPetite does a hefty wedding cake business, in addition to being a full-line bakery selling breakfast items (like bacon buns), cakes, donuts, cookies and pastries. Their version of the atomic cake is called a rainbow cake.

Kim's favorite part of running the bakery is all the customers who return year after year.

"I've got people that drive in from Minnesota just to come here, all the way here to get bacon buns and coffeecakes," she said. "I've got people that come from Indiana and buy thirty coffeecakes at a time. Chocolate chip and apricot are their favorites."

Kim's favorite? The pecan coffeecake.

SICILIA BAKERY

5939 West Lawrence Avenue in Jefferson Park

Joe Pecoraro, the founder of Sicilia Bakery, got his start in the baking business when he was only ten years old. He lived in Bagheria, Sicily, at the time, training alongside two powerhouse Sicilian bakers: Michele Di Paolo and Toto Fucarino, at Pasticceria La Favorita bakery. By the time Pecoraro immigrated to the United States in 1965, he was already an accomplished baker.

Three years after arriving, in 1968, Pecoraro and his wife, Roselia, opened their own spot, Sicilia Bakery. The cases are full of more than just Sicilian treats, though. Pecoraro decided to include baked goods from all of Italy—think cannoli, cookies, biscotti, zeppole and scratch-made bread. The cannoli are so popular that they were featured on television as one of

Chicago's best. Sicilia offers a slate of savory goods as well, including the popular New Orleans muffuletta sandwich—the inventor of which was also a Sicilian baker.

> Fred Pecoraro on the Dying Breed of Scratch-Made Bakeries
>
> We have people that call in from all over the country now that they've moved out, wanting to know if we're still here in the area and how much they appreciate the fact that we're still here. They can't get this quality food in other states that they've moved to, so now we're shipping stuff out to people all over the country. [Scratch bakeries are] a dying breed. It feels like the whole corporate food world is taking over everything and leveling the flavors. Everything's just bland. [People] just want convenience, and they want it to be fast, and they want to be in and out. It's really sad. [But] bakeries are still necessary. I'm hoping that people still continue on with the traditions that their grandparents and parents brought along.

Today, the Percoraros' son Fred runs the bakery. Under his leadership, Sicilia has also opened a sandwich shop in the Logan Square neighborhood called Rosie's Sidekick—named after Fred's mother, Roselia. Joe is eighty and still comes in the bakery every day to work. Customers regularly come in as well, telling stories of how Sicilia made their wedding cake and their parents' wedding cake or sharing memories of when a slice of Sicilian pizza at the bakery was only thirty-five cents.

"I was lucky," Fred said. "I was a little kid, and I got to work in a bakery. As kids, me and my sisters, my mom, my dad, we were all here. We all worked together. I've been pretty lucky to experience the things I got to experience being in a family business, everything from meeting people to making people smile and be happy. I don't think you would get that experience anywhere else. I don't think there's a college that can teach you that."

As of June 2021, Pecoraro plans to rent out the Sicilia space and begin running a bakery food truck in its place.

AMBER BAKERY

2326 East 71st Street in South Shore

Amber Bakery was a staple in southern Chicago with multiple locations throughout its run. Fritz Puetter opened the bakery as an adult, in 1969, after he came to the South Shore neighborhood from Germany when he was just fourteen. He ran it for eleven years, winning locals over with frosted yellow cakes, cookies, whipped cream cakes and blueberry muffins. Puetter retired in 1980 and sold the bakery to his son Frederick. From there it passed to one more family member, who eventually sold it to someone outside the family; it closed for good just a few years later.

MIARA'S BAKERY, DELI AND LIQUOR STORE

7051–53 West Addison Street in Dunning

For several decades, Miara's Bakery sold some of the highest rated Polish desserts in the city—plus deli meat, beer and liquor. The business was mostly known for baked goods, though. Most famous was the kolacz (pronounced ko-wotz), an eggy bread made with raisins and a baked-on creamy cheese topping. Miara's was also well known for cookies, cheesecakes and pączki. The pączki, filled with custard or jam, often sold out by noon.

D'AMATO'S BAKERY

1124 West Grand Avenue in the West Loop

With most family bakeries, the secrets of the trade are passed down from parent to child through the generations. Not so with D'Amato's Bakery. At this Italian bread bakery, the knowledge went from son to father.

In 1961, Nicola D'Amato immigrated to Chicago from Adelfia, Italy. His entire family—a wife and three sons—came to the United States with him. When they arrived, Nicola went to work in construction. His wife, Rosa, became a seamstress, and his oldest son, Matteo, took a job two doors down from their home at Italian French Bakery.

Italian French Bakery opened in 1912 and specialized in Italian French bread, which is Italian bread in longer, narrower loaves, like French bread. The oven was coal-fired. In 1971, ten years after Nicola, Rose and the family came to Chicago, Matteo's boss at Italian French Bakery wanted to retire. He encouraged Nicola to buy the shop. They inked the deal, Matteo taught the entire family to bake bread, and the shop was renamed to D'Amato's Bakery.

FROM MIARA'S RECIPE BOX

Cheese Kolacz

(as told to The Catholic Charities Keenager News*)*

Bread Ingredients

4 tablespoons butter
½ cup sugar
1 teaspoon salt
½ teaspoon allspice (optional)
1 cup milk, scalded
1 package active dry yeast
¼ cup lukewarm water
3 eggs
5 cups flour
1 cup raisins

Topping Ingredients

2 cups dry cottage cheese or farmer's cheese
2 eggs
3 tablespoons sugar
¼ teaspoon salt
8 ounces cream cheese

Directions

Place butter, sugar, salt, allspice and milk in a large mixing bowl. Let cool to lukewarm. In a small bowl, soften yeast in lukewarm water. Add yeast to milk mixture. Beat in eggs, add half of the flour and heat until smooth. Add raisins and remainder of flour.

Knead dough on a floured surface until it no longer sticks to your hands, about 8 minutes. Place in a greased bowl, cover and let rise until doubled, from 1 to 2 hours. Punch dough down and divide in half. Pat into 2 9-inch cast-iron skillets or cake pans. Combine topping ingredients and beat until smooth. Spread over coffeecakes. Cover and let rise again until doubled, about 1 hour. Bake in preheated 350 oven for 1 hour.

Now, D'Amato's is a West Loop staple, known still for fresh-baked bread. It also gained fame for cannoli, Sicilian-style pizza, zeppole, sfogliatelle and chocolate-dipped cookies. In 2012, the bakery started selling sandwiches, too. One of the local favorite items is the Big Cannoli, a single giant cannolo stuffed with about forty mini cannoli. And everything is still baked in that same coal-fired oven from 1912. D'Amato's gets a coal delivery every day from Indiana. They burn the coal for five to seven hours, then close all the chimneys and use the residual heat to bake their food. The bakery is one of only two coal-fired shops in the city; the other is a pizza place.

Victor D'Amato, Nicola's son and Matteo's brother, owns the bakery now. Aside from the storefront, there's a healthy commercial business; they sell bread to more than four hundred restaurants in Chicagoland. No matter where you get your D'Amato's bread, just remember to eat the crust. If you don't, "You're not Italian," Victor says.

OLD FASHIONED DONUTS

11248 South Michigan Avenue in Roseland

At eighty-two years old as of this writing, Old Fashioned Donuts' owner Buritt Bulloch still comes into work every day for a full thirteen and a half hours to make donuts from scratch, just like he's been doing since he opened his shop in 1972. He's been making donuts in Roseland for so long that customers now call him the Donut King. They love his Long Johns, apple fritters, bismarcks, glazed donuts and Texas donuts (ones that are four times larger than a normal donut). Bulloch's shop is so popular that on weekdays, he sells about two hundred dozen donuts, and about three hundred dozen on the weekends. The favorite by far is the glazed donut.

"Around here, when you're out of glazed, you're out of donuts as far as they're concerned," Bulloch told ABC 7 News.

Bulloch moved to Chicago from Mississippi in the 1960s. He worked at two other donut shops before opening his; the owner of the second shop suggested Bulloch buy it, but at that point he already had a following of his own. When he opened his shop, there were a few other mom-and-pop bakeries on the block as well. None of them lasted, but Old Fashioned Donuts remains in place.

Bulloch's daughters, nephew and granddaughter help out in the shop now, and they will take over when—or if—Bulloch retires.

Bibliography

Abbott, N. "Throwback Thursday—Burny Brothers, Inc." Epstein. https://www.epsteinglobal.com/news/throwback-thursday-burny-brothers-inc

ABC7. "Allegretti's Carrying on Sicilian Tradition." https://abc7chicago.com/archive/8584552/.

ABC13. "Reuter's Bakery Poundcakes Worth the Calories." https://abc13.com/archive/9090037/.

Baker, R.S. "Capital and Labor Hunt Together: Chicago the Victim of the New Industrial Conspiracy." *McClure's*, September 1903.

Bays Corporation. "Celebrate 80 Years with Bays English Muffins." Cision. https://www.prnewswire.com/news-releases/celebrate-80-years-with-bays-english-muffins-300006706.html.

Bays English Muffins. "About Us." https://bays.com/about-bays.

Beckwith, Lynn. "Books Reviews: Sing a Song of Tuna Fish by Esmé Raji Codell." BookPage. https://bookpage.com/reviews/3913-esme-raji-codell-esmes-childhood-memories-childrens.

Berghold, G.J. "Dedicated to Austrian-Hungarian Burgenland Family History." *Burgenland Bunch News*. https://www.the-burgenland-bunch.org/Newsletter/NL/Newsletter%20118.htm.

Bielinski, D., H. Fingerhut, H. Hanson and E. Hanson. *Sweets: Desserts That Went to Market*. Panel. April 5, 2008. https://www.wbez.org/stories/sweets-desserts-that-went-to-market/ca2a9283-cb6c-4768-8f62-938f7c0ce057.

Bizzarri, A. "Frosty Italian Treat Traces Chicago Roots to 1 Family.: *Chicago Tribune*. Retrieved May 30, 2021. https://digitaledition.chicagotribune.com/tribune/article_popover.aspx?guid=ef253699-9c87-4ad6-865b-d100de3294f9.

Bong, B. "Comings & Goings: Tuzik's Bakery Closes in Oak Lawn." *Chicago Tribune*, November 19, 2019. https://www.chicagotribune.com/suburbs/daily-southtown/ct-sta-comings-goings-st-1121-20191119-3fhpdk2qibecjbol67w3tg7mpe-story.html.

Boston Globe. "Janina Doktor Obituary (2013)." Legacy. https://www.legacy.com/amp/obituaries/bostonglobe/163049895.

Boyer, J. "Turano Goes Back to Its Pizza Roots." *Wednesday Journal*, February 11, 2021. https://www.oakpark.com/2008/07/15/turano-goes-back-to-its-pizza-roots/.

Breslin, M.M. "Alice Versecky, Berwyn Bakery Owner." *Chicago Tribune*, August 30, 2018. https://www.chicagotribune.com/news/ct-xpm-1998-08-08-9808080153-story.html.

Bruno, K. "FOOD: Monroe's Holey Trinity." *Jackson (MS) Free Press*, March 3, 2003. https://www.jacksonfreepress.com/news/2003/mar/03/food-monroes-holey-trinity/.

Bureau of Alcohol, Tobacco, Firearms and Explosives. "Eliot Ness: Special Agent Eliot Ness, a Legacy ATF Agent." https://www.atf.gov/our-history/eliot-ness.

Calumet Bakery. https://calumetbakery.com.

Cantrell, W. "Family Bakery Part of the Neighborhood." *Chicago Tribune*, September 3, 2018. https://www.chicagotribune.com/news/ct-xpm-1990-07-25-9003030425-story.html.

Carlozo, L. "Chicago's Lutz Bakery Takes the Cake after Food Network Episode." AOL. https://www.aol.com/2010/07/13/chicagos-lutz-bakery-takes-the-cake-after-food-network-episode/.

CBS Chicago. "Chicago Anti-Valentine's Day Guide." https://chicago.cbslocal.com/top-lists/chicago-anti-valentine%E2%80%99s-day-guide/.

———. "End of an Era: Naples Bakery Closes, After 97 Years in Business." https://chicago.cbslocal.com/2016/12/31/end-of-an-era-naples-bakery-closes-after-97-years-in-business/.

Chen, S. "Meet Baumkuchen, Germany's Glorious Cake on a Spit." Popsugar Food. https://www.popsugar.com/food/What-Baumkuchen-23064166.

Chicago Austin News. "Employees Throw Party on Burny's Anniversary." January 20, 1960. https://newspaperarchive.com/celebrity-clipping-jan-20-1960-984491/.

Chicago Italian Beef. "The Origins and Growth of Turano Bakery." https://chicagoitalianbeef.com/blog/the-origins-and-growth-of-turano-bakery.

Chicago Reader. "D'Amato's #1 Italian and French Bakery." https://www.chicagoreader.com/chicago/damatos-1-italian-and-french-bakery/Location?oid=1024398.

Chicago South End Reporter. July 28, 1943. https://newspaperarchive.com/chicago-south-end-reporter-jul-28-1943-p-1/.

Chicago's Best. "Chicago's Best Italian: D'Amato's Bakery." https://wgntv.com/chicagosbesttv/chicagos-best-italian-damatos-bakery/.

Chicago Sun Times. "Henrietta 'Hank' Buoniconti." Legacy. https://legacy.suntimes.com/amp/obituaries/chicagosuntimes/20432005.

———. "Jacob W. Wagner obituary." Legacy. https://legacy.suntimes.com/obituaries/chicagosuntimes/obituary.aspx?n=jacob-w-wagner&pid=2536728&fhid=2045.

Chicago Tribune. "Audrey Hopfner-Hurley." June 3, 2003. https://www.chicagotribune.com/news/ct-xpm-2003-06-03-0306030193-story.html.

———. "Bakery Closed after Mice Droppings Found." August 24, 2018. https://www.chicagotribune.com/news/ct-xpm-2008-04-07-0804070173-story.html.

———. "Edna Ida Heck." April 7, 2000. https://www.chicagotribune.com/news/ct-xpm-2000-04-07-0004070288-story.html.

———. "Emilia Albano." February 22, 1987. https://www.chicagotribune.com/news/ct-xpm-1987-02-22-8701150087-story.html

———. "Ethnic Bakeries Spark Reader Memories." August 6, 2003. https://www.chicagotribune.com/news/ct-xpm-2003-08-06-0308060126-story.html.

———. "Fritz Puetter." December 18, 1987. https://www.chicagotribune.com/news/ct-xpm-1987-12-18-8704040026-story.html

———. "Howard M. Hackel." Legacy. https://www.legacy.com/us/obituaries/chicagotribune/name/howard-hackel-obituary?id=2393237.

———. "Jule F. Burny. (2007)." Legacy. https://www.legacy.com/us/obituaries/chicagotribune/name/jule-burny-obituary?pid=94310539.

———. "Raymond M. Hoeffken." February 4, 1987. https://www.chicagotribune.com/news/ct-xpm-1987-02-04-8701090631-story.html.

———. "U.S. Raids Bakery; 12 Poles Detained." February 13, 1986. https://www.chicagotribune.com/news/ct-xpm-1986-02-13-8601110739-story.html.

———. "William Reynen Obituary." Legacy. https://www.legacy.com/us/obituaries/chicagotribune/name/william-reynen-obituary?pid=180202646.

Chowhound. "Norbert Blei's 'Neighborhood' (Vesecky's, Bohemian Chicago, Old School Baking)." https://www.chowhound.com/post/norbert-bleis-neighborhood-veseckys-bohemian-chicago-school-113622.

Chronicling Illinois. Herman H. Kohlsaat Collection. Abraham Lincoln Presidential Library & Museum. http://alplm-cdi.com/chroniclingillinois/collections/show/461.

Chu, L. "Bridgeport Bakery Closing on Halloween after 78 Years." *Chicago Tribune*, October 11, 2019. https://www.chicagotribune.com/dining/ct-food-bridgeport-bakery-south-side-closing-paczki-1011-20191011-6nmz6l4fcfcpthyj4374zyhpr4-story.html

———. "Swedish Bakery in Andersonville Closing after 88 Years." February 3, 2017. https://www.chicagotribune.com/dining/ct-swedish-bakery-in-andersonville-closing-after-88-years-20170202-story.html.

Clark, B. "State & Union: Going Crackers at Manny Hanny." *Olean Times Herald*, August 20, 2020. https://www.oleantimesherald.com/news/state-union-going-crackers-at-manny-hanny/article_a99db15b-acac-5ff2-aeab-a78327415e17.html.

Cohen, S. "Café Draws Newcomers to Pullman." *South Side Weekly*, November 3, 2015. https://southsideweekly.com/cafe-draws-newcomers-to-pullman/.

Connolly, D. "Naples Bakery to Close Its Doors after 97 Years." The Reporter Online, November 17, 2016. https://thereporteronline.net/?p=68640

Cormier-Pellerin, C. "Fresh Is Better: Bay English Muffins." *Business In Focus*, August 2018. https://www.businessinfocusmagazine.com/2018/08/fresh-is-better.

Countryside Funeral Homes & Crematory. "Obituary for William Bell." https://memorials.countrysidefuneralhomes.com/Beil-William/3407322/obituary.php.

Craven, K. "Northwest Side Baker Johann Kaes, 31." *Chicago Tribune*, May 19, 1999. https://www.chicagotribune.com/news/ct-xpm-1999-05-19-9905190266-story.html

Dailey, P. "Bohemian Bounty." *Chicago Tribune*, October 21, 1993. https://www.chicagotribune.com/news/ct-xpm-1993-10-21-9310210348-story.html.

Daley, B. "Remembrance of Sugar Cookies Past." *Chicago Tribune*, March 6, 2012. https://www.chicagotribune.com/lifestyles/ct-xpm-2012-03-06-ct-tribu-daley-question-sugar-cookies-20120306-story.html.

Dallas (TX) Express. January 13, 1900.

Damato's Chicago. "D'Amato's—Bakery & Subs." https://damatoschicago.com/.

DeGrechie, E. "Leonard's Bakery Closing after 34 Years in Northbrook." Patch. https://patch.com/illinois/northbrook/leonards-bakery-closing-after-34-years-northbrook.

Demarest, E. "El Nopal Bakery, Little Village 'Pioneer,' Closes After 60-Plus Years." DNAinfo Chicago, August 13, 2015. https://www.dnainfo.com/chicago/20150813/little-village/el-nopal-bakery-little-village-pioneer-closes-after-60-plus-years.

———. "El Nopal Bakery Reopens in Little Village." DNAinfo Chicago, October 27, 2017. https://www.dnainfo.com/chicago/20171027/little-village/el-nopal-open-family-bakery-francisco-celia-frank-bonilla/.

Dispatch-Argus. "Muffin Masters a Chicago Fixture Since 1933." July 29, 1999. https://qconline.com/news/illinois/muffin-masters-a-chicago-fixture-since-1933/article_f9790aa2-487d-53db-8395-71d395baa4f8.html.

Dolinsky, S. "Italian Bakery—A Tradition Worth Traveling For." Steve Dolinsky, January 22, 2011. https://stevedolinsky.com/tasty-bakery-tradition-worth-traveling-for.

Donato, M. "Ann Fingerhut, Ex-Bakery Owner." *Chicago Tribune*, August 30, 2018. https://www.chicagotribune.com/news/ct-xpm-1997-08-25-9708250157-story.html.

D'Onofrio, J. "Andersonville's Swedish Bakery, in Business for 88 Years, Opens for Last Time Fat Tuesday." ABC7 Chicago. https://abc7chicago.com/swedish-bakery-chicago-andersonville-closing/1777065/.

Eating the World. "D'Amato's, An Old School Italian Bakery on West Grand Avenue." https://eatingtheworld.net/2015/04/13/damatos-an-old-school-italian-bakery-on-west-grand-avenue/.

Edgewater Historical Society. "All in the Family." http://www.edgewaterhistory.org/ehs/articles/v06-1-3.

———. "V28-1 Swedish Bakery Closes after 38 Years." http://www.edgewaterhistory.org/ehs/content/v28-1-swedish-bakery-closes-after-38-years.

Enna, R. "Tradition Rises to the Occasion at Bakery." *Chicago Tribune*, March 19, 1997. (https://www.chicagotribune.com/news/ct-xpm-1997-03-19-9703190246-story.html.

Facebook. "Growing up in Chicago." from https://www.facebook.com/Growing-up-in-Chicago-325488420983547.

———. "Vanished Chicagoland." Retrieved May 28, 2021. https://www.facebook.com/vanishedchicagoland.

Fleischer, D. "Retired Baker Gets Ready to Celebrate 100th Birthday." Journal & Topics, January 4, 2018. https://www.journal-topics.com/articles/retired-baker-gets-ready-to-celebrate-100th-birthday/.

Food Network. (n.d.). *All of the Pizza: A Regional Pizza Style Guide*. https://www.foodnetwork.com/recipes/packages/italian-cooking-basics/all-of-the-pizza-a-regional-pizza-style-guide.

Forgotten Chicago Forum. "Little Village Hobby Stores on 26th Street that Sold Model Kits. Bakeries." https://forgottenchicago.com/forum/read.php?1,8655.

Fra Noi. "County Board Celebrates Lezza's Sweet Success." https://franoi.com/food/lezza/.

The Fresh Loaf. "English Muffin Recipe Like Bays." https://www.thefreshloaf.com/node/39980/english-muffin-recipe-bays.

Gale, N. "The Fingerhut Bakery Was a Chicago Staple Since 1895." Digital Research Library of Illinois History Journal. https://drloihjournal.blogspot.com/2018/09/the-fingerhut-bakery-was-a-chicago-staple-since-1895.html.

———. "Lutz Café and Pastry Shop of Chicago, Illinois." Digital Research Library of Illinois History Journal. https://drloihjournal.blogspot.com/2019/05/lutz-cafe-and-pastry-shop-of-chicago-illinois.html.

———. "39 Chicago-Style Foods Explained, Including Photographs." Digital Research Library of Illinois History Journal. https://drloihjournal.blogspot.com/2019/12/chicago-style-foods-explained.html.

Gebert, M. "'I Was Always a Deli Shlepper': Owner Bette Dworkin on Why She Had to Bring Kaufman's Deli Back." Grub Street. https://www.grubstreet.com/2012/12/kaufmans-deli-bette-dworkin-interview.html.

Grave, J. "Hidden in Plain Sight: Alliance Bakery." BYT // Brightest Young Things. https://brightestyoungthings.com/articles/hidden-in-plain-sight-alliance-bakery.

Gunderson, E. "Ask Geoffrey: Sept. 2." WTTW News. https://news.wttw.com/2015/09/02/ask-geoffrey-sept-2.

Harrell, A. "Garfield & Wabash." *South Side Weekly*, February 11, 2016. https://southsideweekly.com/garfield-wabash.

Harvey (IL) Tribune. June 26, 1931. https://newspaperarchive.com/harvey-tribune-jun-26-1931-p-2/.

Hayes, N. "Alegretti's Bakery Preps for St. Joseph's Day Rush." *Chicago Tribune*, March 12, 2015. https://www.chicagotribune.com/suburbs/norridge/ct-nhh-algrettis-ms-tl-0312-20150309-story.html.

Healy, V.O. "Recall an Era when Dressel's Cake Reigned." *Chicago Tribune*, January 8, 2010. https://www.chicagotribune.com/news/ct-xpm-2010-01-08-1001060531-story.html

Heise, K. "Ernest Dorner, 79: Bakery Co-Owner." *Chicago Tribune*, March 2, 1993. https://www.chicagotribune.com/news/ct-xpm-1993-03-02-9303186575-story.html.

———. "Helene Reynen, 89: Owner Old-Fashioned Bakery." *Chicago Tribune*, May 16, 1996. https://www.chicagotribune.com/news/ct-xpm-1996-05-16-9605160148-story.html.

———. "James Bay Sr.; Led English Muffin Firm." *Chicago Tribune*, April 3, 1997. https://www.chicagotribune.com/news/ct-xpm-1997-04-03-9704030311-story.html.

Herringshaw, C.J. *Clark J. Herringshaw's City Blue Book of Current Biography: Chicago Men of 1913; An Alphabetical Record of Citizens Prominent in Their Chosen Vocations in Chicago's Educational, Social, Civil, Industrial and Commercial Affairs*. Chicago: American Publishers' Association, 1913.

Hill, R.A., and M. Garvey. *The Marcus Garvey and Universal Negro Improvement Association Papers*, vol. 3. *September 1920–August 1921*. Berkeley: University of California Press, 1984.

Holton, J. "The Early Bird Catches The (Ear)worm #socs." The Sound of One Hand Typing. https://thesoundofonehandtyping.com/2021/04/03/the-early-bird-catches-the-earworm-socs.

Illinois General Assembly. "Full Text of HR0022." https://www.ilga.gov/legislation/fulltext.asp?DocName=&SessionId=85&GA=98&DocTypeId=HR&DocNum=22&GAID=12&LegID=71264&SpecSess=&Session=.

———. "Full Text of HR1612." https://www.ilga.gov/legislation/fulltext.asp?DocName=09500HR1612lv&SessionID=51&GA=95&DocTypeID=HR&DocNum=1612&SpecSess=&Session=&print=true.

Inserra, V.L. *C-1 and the Chicago Mob*. N.p.: Xlibris, 2014.

INSP TV. "State Plate." *Episode 2: Illinois*. https://www.insp.com/presskit/state-plate/episodes/episode-2-illinois/.

Isabella County (MI) Enterprise. February 5, 1886.

justjoan. "Fingurhut Bakery." *Chicago Food Chat* (blog). LTHForum.com, February 29, 2008. https://www.lthforum.com/bb/viewtopic.php?t=18125.

Kadushin, R. "48 Hours Chicago: The Best of a City in Two Days." *National Geographic*. https://www.nationalgeographic.com/traveler/articles/1103chicago.html.

Karla Sullivan. "Amber Bakery and Dressels." https://karlasullivandotcom.wordpress.com/2019/09/02/amber-bakery-and-dressels/.

Keegan, A. "Deli Triumphs Over Twin Dose of Salmonella." *Chicago Tribune*, May 19, 1986. https://www.chicagotribune.com/news/ct-xpm-1986-05-19-8602040923-story.html.

Konkol, Mark. "*Plan for New Pullman Cafe Might Not Sound Like a Big Deal… But It Is*." *My Chicago* (blog), May 20, 2015. DNAinfo. https://www.dnainfo.com/chicago/20150520/pullman/plan-for-new-pullman-cafe-might-not-sound-like-big-deal-but-it-is.

LaGrave, K. "7 Cannoli Hotspots in the U.S." Showbiz Cheat Sheet. https://www.cheatsheet.com/life/7-cannoli-hotspots-in-the-u-s.html/

La Petite Pastry. http://www.lapetitepastry.com/default.aspx.

Legacy. "Edward A. Haas." https://www.legacy.com/amp/obituaries/dailyherald/164454058.

Letter from Elba. "Piece of Cake." https://www.letterfromelba.com/piece-of-cake.

Levy, C. "Cleaning Out Library Leftovers from the Cold War." UIC Today. https://today.uic.edu/cleaning-out-library-leftovers-from-the-cold-war

Lewis, L., and H.J. Smith. *Chicago: The History of Its Reputation*. New York: Harcourt, Brace and Company, 1929.

Lost Recipes Found. "The Story of Dressel's Whipped Cream Cake." YouTube video. May 8, 2012. https://www.youtube.com/watch?v=1_an0P5uZUA&ab_channel=lostrecipesfound.

LTH—Chicago's Food Chat Community. https://www.lthforum.com.

Mahany, B. "They Just Don't Bake 'Em Like This Anymore." *Chicago Tribune*, March 6, 1993. https://www.chicagotribune.com/news/ct-xpm-1994-03-06-9403060224-story.html.

Mann, Leslie. "Small Town with Prices to Match." *Chicago Tribune*, March 29, 2013. https://www.chicagotribune.com/real-estate/ct-home-0329-northlake-profile-20130329-story.html.

Marcus & Millichap. *Los Feliz Mixed Used-Retail & Office Owner-User/ Value-Add Investment Opportunity*. https://images1.cityfeet.com/d2/Cle-em5fxudY_JPCKSZpRziHfAw1Mq1GDRhorhRQEoY/document.pdf

Marshall K. "Connie's Beef North & Narragansett." *Chicago Food Chat* (blog). LTHForum.com, January 21, 2009. https://www.lthforum.com/bb/viewtopic.php?f=14&t=22594.

Martello, C. J. "Random Roseland Memories." Fra Noi. https://franoi.com/petals/random-roseland-memories.

Mathius, E. "Interview with Al Davino about Italian Bakeries, Chicago, Illinois, Part 1." May 11, 1977. Library of Congress. https://www.loc.gov/item/afc1981004_afs20730b/.

———. "Interview with Alfonso Davino, Baker, Chicago, Illinois." May 5, 1997. Library of Congress. https://www.loc.gov/item/afc1981004_afs20718a/.

McGhee, J. "The Early Days of Andersonville's Swedish Bakery." DNAinfo. https://www.dnainfo.com/chicago/20170221/andersonville/early-days-of-andersonvilles-swedish-bakery.

Midson, L. "Smashburger, Live Basil and Tom's Urban Chef Andrew Selvaggio." Westword. https://www.westword.com/restaurants/smashburger-live-basil-and-toms-urban-chef-andrew-selvaggio-you-dont-learn-a-trade-you-steal-it-5726721.

Mills, M. "Bakeries Leaven Two Melting-Pot Neighborhoods." *Chicago Tribune*, February 5, 1986. https://www.chicagotribune.com/news/ct-xpm-1986-02-05-8601100126-story.html.

Monroes Donuts and Bakery. "*Keeping the Vision Alive*." https://monroesdonutsandbakery.com/co-history/.

Morris, J. "The Legacy of Schulze Baking Company, Part 1." Chicago Patterns. http://chicagopatterns.com/the-legacy-of-schulze-baking-company-part-1/.

Myers, Q. "'Chicago Tonight' in Your Neighborhood: Bridgeport." WTTW News. https://news.wttw.com/2021/04/08/chicago-tonight-your-neighborhood-bridgeport.

My Italian Family Recipe. "Italian Ice (Recipe)." https://www.cook-italian.com/weblog/2009/05/italian-ice.html?cid=6a010535d7df4f970b012876e07bc2970c#comment-6a010535d7df4f970b012876e07bc2970c.

Nadig, B. "Gladstone Park Bakery Site Up For Sale." Nadig Newspapers. http://nadignewspapers.com/2017/04/04/gladstone-park-bakery-site-up-for-sal.

National Labor Relations Board, Petitioner, v. Augusta Bakery Corporation, Respondent. United States Court of Appeals, Seventh Circuit. March 24, 1992.

New York Age. January 1, 1914. http://www.newspapers.com/newspage/33462429/.

Nineteenth Century. The Magazine of the Victorian Society in America, Fall 2020. http://victoriansociety.org/upload/NC-40-2.pdf.

Northwest Indiana Small Business Development Center. "Fingerhut Family." E-Day Leaders. https://edayleaders.com/eday-winners/fingerhut-family/.

Ori, R. "Pompei Founder's Grandsons in Battle Over Use of Name." Crain's Chicago Business, August 1, 2013. https://www.chicagobusiness.com/article/20130801/CRED03/130809985/pompei-founder-s-grandsons-in-battle-over-use-of-name.

Our Lady of the Angels Fire Memorial. "Personal Experiences with Our Lady of the Angels School Fire on December 1, 1958." https://www.olafire.com/Story.asp?S=67.

Pallasch, A.M. "Customers Call Bakery's Closing Hard to Swallow." *Chicago Tribune*, January 11, 1999. https://www.chicagotribune.com/news/ct-xpm-1999-01-11-9901110076-story.html.

People v. Gallo, 260 ill. App. 3d 1032. Retrieved May 28, 2021. https://casetext.com/case/people-v-gallo-53.

Piltaver, B. "Allegretti's Bakery Celebrates 50 Years in Business!" *People & Places*, January 1, 2013. https://peopleandplacesnewspaper.com/allegrettis-bakery-celebrates-50-years-in-business/.

Pisano, M. "The Sicilian Bakery in Chicago Has Zeppole Delicious and Ready for St. Joseph's Day." *Hardcore Italians* (blog), February 28, 2021. https://hardcoreitalians.blog/2021/02/28/the-sicilian-bakery-in-chicago-has-zeppole-delicious-and-ready-for-st-josephs-day/.

Pullman History Site. https://www.pullman-museum.org/.

punditWeb. "Did Bays English Muffins Change Their Recipe?" https://punditweb.com/did-bays-english-muffins-change-their-recipe/.

Rammohan, Y. "Polish Bakery Fire." WTTW News, September 13, 2011. https://news.wttw.com/2011/09/13/polish-bakery-fire.

Reuter's Bakery. "History." https://www.reutersbakery.com/history/.

Roberts, N. "Best of Bridgeport 2020." *South Side Weekly*, November 29, 2020. https://southsideweekly.com/best-of-bridgeport-2020.

Sherlock, B. "Nicola D'Amato, 77." *Chicago Tribune*, August 27, 2018. https://www.chicagotribune.com/news/ct-xpm-2004-12-30-0412300313-story.html.

Sicilian Bakery Inc. https://sicilianbakeryinc.com.

Smith, D. "Snack Company to Open Searcy Plant." Arkansas Online, March 12, 2009. https://www.arkansasonline.com/news/2009/mar/13/snack-company-open-searcy-plant-20090313.

South Holland (IL) Star. August 4, 1996. https://newspaperarchive.com/south-holland-star-aug-04-1996-p-12/.

Sperling, H. "Classic Takeout: D'Amato's Bakery." Tasting Table, September 6, 2012. https://www.tastingtable.com/cook/chicago/DAmatos-Bakery-Introduces-Sandwiches--Chicago.

St. Frances Xavier Cabrini School. https://saintfrancesxaviercabrini.wordpress.com/st-frances-xavier-cabrini-chicago-illinois/.

Steinberg, N. "Flashback 2009: Lezza Spumoni: Bellwood Ice Cream Legend Started in Little Italy." *Every Goddamn Day* (blog), September 20, 2018. http://www.everygoddamnday.com/2018/09/flashback-2009-lezza-spumoni-treat-that.html

Stetson, Everett. "A Stroll Down the Avenue." Edgewater Historical Society. http://www.edgewaterhistory.org/ehs/articles/v06-1-2.

Stories, L. "Meet Anthony Rubino of Sicilian Bakery in Northwest Side." *Voyage Chicago*, March 6, 2018. http://voyagechicago.com/interview/meet-anthony-rubino-sicilian-bakery-northwest-side.

Sunday Press Books. https://sundaypressbooks.com/nxbook.php.

Sun Sentinel. "Ben Neiman obituary." Legacy. https://www.legacy.com/obituaries/sunsentinel/obituary.aspx?n=ben-neiman&pid=1797279.

Swanson, L. "Oak Lawn Bakery Owner Ted Tuzik Dies Unexpectedly at Age 68." *Patch* (Oak Lawn, Illinois), November 4, 2019. https://patch.com/illinois/oaklawn/oak-lawn-bakery-owner-ted-tuzik-dies-suddenly-age-68.

Tribute Archive. "Eleanor Beil." https://www.tributearchive.com/obituaries/9529208/Eleanor-Beil.

Tricia's Bake Shop. "About Us." https://triciasbakeshop.com/about.

Try Something Fun. "Authentic Old-Time Chicago: Vesecky's Bakery." http://trysomethingfun.com/chicago-veseckys-bakery/.

Turano Baking Co. "Our Story." https://turano.com/story.

U.S. Federal Trade Commission. *Federal Trade Commission Decisions*. Washington, D.C.: U.S. Government Printing Office, 1967.

Vickroy, D. "'Arrivederci,' Naples Bakery in Evergreen Park." *Chicago Tribune*, November 23, 2016. https://www.chicagotribune.com/suburbs/daily-southtown/ct-sta-vickroy-naples-bakery-st-1114-20161115-column.html

Virtusio, J. "Benton Street Bakery Cafe Has Vintage Feel, Down-Home Flavors." *Chicago Tribune*, April 28, 2017. https://www.chicagotribune.com/suburbs/post-tribune/ct-sta-dining-south-benton-st-0428-20170420-story.html.

Watkins, B. "'Donut Man' Who Ran for Jackson Mayor Dreams Big." *Mississippi Clarion Ledger*, August 17, 2017. https://eu.clarionledger.com/story/magnolia/2017/08/17/mayors-race-behind-him-donut-man-dreams-big/571670001/.

WGNTV. "Chicago's Best Bakeries 2: Allegretti's Bakery." December 14, 2015. https://wgntv.com/chicagosbesttv/chicagos-best-bakeries-2-allegrettis-bakery.

Wm. H. Scott Funeral Home. "In Memory of Carl Beil." http://wm-h-scott.tributes.com/dignitymemorial/obituary/Carl-H.-Beil-104433777.

Wright, S. "Scafuri Bakery." Chicago Reader. https://www.chicagoreader.com/chicago/scafuri-bakery/Location?oid=9934428.

Index

C

D

E

F

G

H

I

J

K

L

O

P

R

S

T

U

V

W

Z

About the Author

Jennifer Billock is an award-winning writer, bestselling author, editor and owner of the boutique editorial firm Jennifer Billock Creative Services. She has worked with businesses and publishers, including the Smithsonian, *The New York Times*, National Geographic Traveler, Disney Books, *The Atlantic*, Kraft Foods, *Midwest Living*, Arcadia Publishing and the MSU Press. She is currently dreaming of an around-the-world trip with her Boston terrier. Check out her website at www.jenniferbillock.com and follow her on Twitter @jenniferbillock.

Visit us at
www.historypress.com